Under the Night Sky:
A FATHER'S STORY OF LOVE AND LOSS

STEVEN F. STINGLEY

To our family

And to the memory of
Steven Graham Winter Stingley
(August 7, 1981–February 18, 2005)

"As a child I prayed in my hiding place beneath the roots of an overturned tree that the sight would return to my blind eye. The sight is only enough to see the moon, the rising sun, the blur of stars."
– Jim Harrison, *Prayer*

Monument Rock Press LLC
P.O. Box 311
Monument CO 80132
monumentrock.com

Copyright © 2011 by Steven F. Stingley

ALL RIGHTS RESERVED

Cover art and interior design by Axio Design, Colorado Springs CO

ISBN 978-0615537559 (Custom)
ISBN-10: 0615537553

CONTENTS

Foreword	1
Prologue	6
Promise	13
Phone Calls	19
Winter Morning	23
No Answer	26
A Kiss Good-bye	31
Wondering	34
Dusk	39
Daybreak	45
Fathers and Sons	49
Brother	53
Music in the Chapel	57
Heaven and Earth	62
A Letter from Pops	68
Sympathy Cards	74
From the Guy in the Suit	79
Visit to the Mortuary	83
Cause of Death	88
Into the Desert	91
I Wish	97
What Good am I?	103
Angel with a Ponytail	106
The Ambassade Hotel	111
A Surprise E-mail	114
A Death in Nebraska	120
An Ominous Evening	125
Rain	128
Against Depression	133
Black Dogs and Noonday Demons	137
A Father's Lament	141
Helping Hands	144
The Man on the Sidewalk	151
Visions and Dreams	154
A Baby in August	157
A Father's Love	161
Days on Mount Herman	164
Running Down the Mountain	169
A Young Star	172
Jokerman	176
Marlon Brando of Motown	180
Headaches and Heartaches	184
Final Days	189
Into the Wilderness	192
Above the Wilderness	199
Purple Mountain	203
Purple Mountain Revisited	209
Under the Night Sky	212
Epilogue	217
Photo Gallery	221

ACKNOWLEDGEMENTS

I want to respectfully thank a few special people who have supported me in the past few years and others who have been of particular help in completing this writing project.

First and foremost, I want to acknowledge my wife, Mary, and my sons, Will, Seth, and Colin, all of whom have been endlessly patient, supportive, and loving. So too has been Tara Nooney, Will's fiancée and the mother of our grandson, Walden Graham Stingley. I have the greatest family imaginable.

My parents, Pete and Gloria Stingley, also have been with me every crawl and step of the way, even when some of those steps have not been what they might have expected. They have always given me unquestioning love, and during our time of shared grief, they have been very supportive.

I also want to acknowledge the support of my little sister, Pamela, who always makes me feel better after I talk to her, because she listens to and understands me.

I want to thank countless friends, who have supported me in one important way or another, especially Donovan Anderson, Adam Winter, Dan Winter, Jim Latchaw, and John Whitesides. Additionally, Debbie and Danny Ross, unique friends to our entire family, have supported us with kindness from the early days, and especially since we suffered our loss.

Jerry Mahoney has been of particular help to me, emotionally, philosophically, and creatively. I admire his extensive knowledge of the English language and of the world which the language is intended to describe. And he knows what I have gone through, because he too has lost a son.

I want to acknowledge Deb Cerio, a caring and creative woman I met while taking a class at University of Colorado–Boulder, and in whose Boulder writers group I participated during a particularly critical time for me. That group, and especially Deb, urged me along the way with encouraging words and their passion for writing. Cindy Landsberg of Monument offered the same kind of encouragement and literary counsel, along with a special understanding of loss from her own experience. My project would have never been completed without these two women.

Karl "Duke" Deiotte, Graham's good friend for so many years, also helped me by adding detail to Graham's life and color to his spirit. In many ways, Karl probably knew Graham better than anyone in the years before his death.

Lastly, I want to thank Dr. John Shethar, Mary's therapist who was kind enough to guide me in the years after my loss through my own grieving and creative process. Without his gentle urging and firm hand in helping me set writing deadlines, I would have never completed this book. "Do it to honor Graham," he told me more than once.

I hope that is what I have done.

FOREWORD

December 30, 2011

Picture a collection of forces colliding, intertwining, competing, and you instantly become a participant in Steve Stingley's personal story about the tragic loss of his son, Graham. The colliding forces include family, children, love, clinical depression, helplessness, uncertainty, loss, anguish, grief, support, guilt, childhood memories, and pain. Encouragingly, the negative coalition in that collection is muted a bit by Steve's altruism, courage, hope, and a growing recognition that there is a healing power in becoming a "voice"—a voice that catalyzes others to think, learn, understand, and help. Steve, via this book, mobilizes his voice to help promote greater understanding of what families face in such situations. He helps others. Hopefully, his messages are also aiding his own healing process.

I am a medical doctor, a psychiatrist, neuroscientist, clinician, researcher, and was a long-term chair of the Department of Psychiatry in the University of Michigan Medical School. Relevant to this Foreword,

I am a specialist in clinical depression, the executive director of the University of Michigan Comprehensive Depression Center, the country's inaugural center of excellence in depression, and the chair of the National Network of Depression Centers, which includes 21 of the nation's leading academic centers. Having had a prior friendship with members of Steve's family, I was asked by him to read "Under the Night Sky," his book about Graham. I experienced what most readers will: sadness and empathy for all the Stingleys, and admiration for what Steve has done with this book. In my case, there also was a helplessness that I have come to loathe, and more than a bit of frustration and anger. Why? Because of what I do professionally, whenever I hear about a shortened life due to clinical depression, such as that of Graham Stingley, it angers me.

Some months ago, Steve and I corresponded and spoke about his book. We discovered a trait that we have in common: we write. In his Prologue, he indicated his wish to "... express my memory of (Graham), in the best way I know how: I write." I also write. Steve had read a Foreword I wrote for another book, and asked whether I might do the same for his book. I was honored to accept.

I am asked frequently why the University of Michigan chose to establish a center that specializes in depression, bipolar, and related illnesses. Aware that my detailed answers might bore, I *rapidly* state that depression is a global leader in "burden of disease" and produces more disability than cancer and cardiovascular illnesses combined; that it is second in financial cost among *all* diseases; that it is the most costly source of disability for most corporations and colleges; and, as exemplified by the Stingleys' experiences, it jeopardizes the happiness of entire families and their extended communities. I also point out that clinical depression affects one in every six people, a startling figure, and if bipolar illnesses are added, the figure is one of every five in our lifetimes—one in five. I quickly mention that symptom onset generally starts early in life, peaking between the ages of 15 and 24; that depression has a relentless, episodic, recurrent course if untreated, with a coming-and-going pattern that masquerades its gradual chronic evolution; that it is easier to attack earlier in its course and much, much harder the longer it lasts; that there are known genetic underpinnings; and that stress is a key variable in setting off or worsening episodes. I always seek to interject that depression is a brain disease, that we are learning enough to be able to visualize or image changes in the brain when they occur, and that this single illness—all by itself—is linked with approximately 80 percent of all suicides. The latter comments in some produce what I call the "flinch factor," frowning, silence, and skeptical comments about what depression is. I have come to recognize these as underlying signals of a powerful enemy—stigma, almost always stemming from misunderstandings. If given a few more precious moments, I explain that depression and bipolar illnesses are treatable, at least in most of us, but that 30 percent of those struggling do not respond ideally to our current array of medications, psychotherapies or augmenting treatments. These 30 percent have what is called "Treatment Resistant Depression" or TRD (TRD does not mean the depression is untreatable; it simply denotes that it is *more* difficult to attain and maintain wellness).

The statistics summarized above emerge from thousands of research studies. Such statistics are important but dry. In contrast, Steve's story of Graham is warm, touching, and painful. It hopefully won't escape readers that Graham's experiences classically paralleled depression's usual course. He apparently struggled with the depressive triad of "negative thoughts of self, world, and future." He had altered sleep patterns, headaches and other physical symptoms. Depression starts in the brain, but the entire body is impacted. And he and his family continuously searched for the right treatment, and strategies for dealing with the undesirable side effects that occur all too often. Sadly, another parallel existed for Graham: he was one of the approximate 30 percent whose depression was treatment resistant.

Depression and bipolar illness have pervasive reaches. Steve Stingley, his wife Mary, their other sons and friends all were greatly impacted by Graham's disease. All families familiar with these diseases are. And since it is so common, we *all* need to ask, "What can we do to help conquer these illnesses to prevent others from undergoing similar traumas?" The answers constitute the mission of the University of Michigan's Depression Center: find depression and bipolar illnesses earlier in life; support more research to identify underlying causes and develop better treatments; maintain wellness once achieved, recognizing that recurrences generally occur if treatments are stopped; and bury the stigma that stems from ignorance, once and for all. Knowledge heals, and we have too little. Stigma destroys, and we have too much.

Are we gaining in conquering depression and bipolar illnesses? Yes. Are there prospects of better treatments? Yes. Neuroscience and social science discoveries are unraveling the underlying mysteries. Treatments are getting better. For those whose depressions are most difficult to treat, this cannot occur too soon. And while waiting for breakthroughs, we are learning that we must discard needless arguments about whether one treatment is superior to another and focus on integrating *all* helpful interventions for each individual. These include often-essential medications and psychotherapies, sleep interventions, and newer strategies for modulating brain function. They also include an understanding that depression and bipolar are illnesses, and exercise, love, hugs, positive reminders, animals, writing, siblings, friends, spirituality, and nature—sunshine for some and night skies for others, such as Graham and Steve.

Steve was urged to write about Graham's life, struggles and death by his friends and supporters and to "do it for Graham." Nearing the book's completion he describes observing a Colorado mountain sky ablaze with "a billion stars" and he whispered to himself, "Graham would have loved this." I smiled at Steve's reassuring memory and wished I could have seen that night sky. Because of what I do professionally, I wished even more fervently that Graham had found better answers for his illness so that he could still be enjoying those skies.

We will find better treatments, Graham. We will.

FOREWORD

John F. Greden, M.D.
Rachel Upjohn Professor of Psychiatry and Clinical Neurosciences
Executive Director, University of Michigan Comprehensive Depression Center

Founding Chair, National Network of Depression Centers (NNDC)
Research Professor, Molecular and Behavioral Neuroscience Institute

www.depressioncenter.org
www.NNDC.org
www.med.umich.edu/psych/

"There's matter in these sighs; these profound heaves you must translate; 'tis fit we understand them. Where is your son?"

– Shakespeare, *Hamlet*

PROLOGUE

After a night of working heavily on this book, I crawled into bed, my head spinning. There was so much to tell, to feel, and to think about my son Graham. And the writing only seemed to be unfolding the depths of my loss. There was nowhere to hide; nowhere to find relief.

Reaching for a distraction, I picked up an old, tattered, paperback edition of *Hamlet*. I had tried several times over many years to read this play. But finding Shakespeare difficult, I usually ended up replacing it with a more contemporary book. Now, however, I hoped it would take me away to a different time and place, away from the anguished world inside my head.

Ironically, when I opened the book randomly to find the page where I'd left off last time, the above quote was the first thing I saw. It seemed I could not escape my painful existence; or *our* painful existence. Though the context of the quote was completely different from my situation as I continued to read later, those first words hit me hard. As I struggled to understand what I'd gone through with my son, it seemed I could not get away from my relentless grief, no matter how hard I tried.

Writers far more observant than me, and in times far before mine, knew this. Shakespeare was aware of the "matter" in "sighs." Now I knew as well. As my own chest rose with each breath and lowered with a sigh, it did indeed feel like a "profound heave." I was alive, but my son was not. And yes, I felt the urge to "translate" those heaves, so I could understand them.

So I have written and written in the years since Graham's death, tapping words on my computer keyboard and scribbling in my journals. This sometimes helped me understand—but perhaps as often it did not. Sometimes, as I pondered the ideas and feelings behind the words I'd write, I was left with new questions and few answers. And to make some sense of all the tapping and scribbling, now I have assembled this book—partly to express my personal journey after losing Graham, but also partly to tell the story of his extraordinary, albeit short, life.

My nature has not always lent itself easily to such self-disclosure. I am not normally comfortable with expressing myself, particularly when it comes to emotions. My upbringing emphasized being positive and pragmatic, and downplayed any attempt to dwell upon or even give voice to negative or troubled feelings. Maybe that is why someone recently told me that I speak "both with irony and sincerity at the same time," as if she were on to my reluctant openness, the internal conflict I have between reticence and honesty.

Throughout the grieving process, I've continually asked myself why I should reveal myself—and my son—so intimately. Writing about what I was experiencing seemed good for me, but I didn't want to violate the sacred and private nature of my relationship with Graham, or somehow disrespect or trivialize his life. Even once I was able to overcome these internal objections and begin my writing project in earnest, I struggled to continue and arrive at some sort of completion. Sometimes the task felt too painful; sometimes I felt simply unable and ill-equipped to complete what I had set out to do.

More than once I've declared to myself and others that I wanted to abandon this project and keep these thoughts to myself, either out of simple exasperation or fear of opening up. But those around me sensed my faltering and came to my aid. "Do it for Graham's sake," John Shethar told me. "Do it to carry forward his spirit."

My family patiently added its encouragement. "Steve, I think this is something you need to do for yourself," Mary told me.

"Dad, stick with your project, because it seems this is something you really want to do," my sons added.

And there was the existential necessity to finish the book. "On a project like this, there is no turning back," my friend Jerry Mahoney wrote me.

But in terms of a broader purpose, I hope my story helps others who have suffered this kind of tragic loss. If it does, then I will have accomplished something bigger than merely dealing with my own grief. I will have enabled Graham's own life to matter beyond the circle of family and friends he profoundly touched.

As I read the news of others suffering similar fates, I can now understand all too clearly and vividly what they are going through. Awful, unexpected things happen every day, if not in our own homes, then in our neighborhoods, communities, and world. Mary and I gasped when we heard that the neighbors up the street lost their daughter to suicide after suffering an unshakeable bout of postpartum depression. Not much after that, there was news of another neighbor losing their son in a traffic accident. Then but a year later another block closer, neighbors lose their young son to alcoholism. On a business trip, I pick up the newspaper and read that a mother and her autistic son were run over by a drunk driver as they rode their bicycles down the sidewalk. About the same time, a woman in our own office has her teen-age son taken from her by a drug overdose. I drive to her home on a warm Colorado morning to do what people did for me, knock on her front door and walk into their mournful living room, to say I understand. I can't make it better, I tell her family, but

PROLOGUE

I understand.

All these families share a disbelief and sorrow deeper than they have ever experienced. I know now firsthand what others have suffered, and I hope my story helps them know they are not alone in their grief and search for answers.

As human beings, we are uncomfortably aware that we will suffer loss in our lifetimes. And though we are wired to assume, even to trust, that our children will not die before us, the unnatural and horrific possibility of their premature deaths always lurks in the back of our minds. In 2005, the year Graham died, there were 2.4 million other deaths in America alone. But it took just a single death for the world, as I knew it, to collapse.

As a note to those who read this book, please keep in mind the words that follow are mine alone. This book has been written solely from my point of view. The only time I divert from my internal voice is when I occasionally quote a musician, a poet, a family member, or a friend of Graham's who said something that had meaning either for Graham or me or both. I also quote directly at times from material Graham himself wrote. But I want the reader to be aware that this book is essentially a personal reflection on Graham's life and death and how they affected me.

As a former journalist, I made a conscious decision early on that I would *not* write a book about Graham's life by trying to piece his story together from multiple viewpoints. I would *not* follow my natural professional instinct to interview his brothers, his mother, his friends, and his acquaintances. There would be no attempt to assemble a journalistic version of how the world knew Graham. The method that had served me so well in journalism— removing myself and my personal judgments and feelings; reporting the facts as best I could; recording life through personal detachment—would not be adequate for me now. There was more to tell.

So this is a different kind of book. This is a book about how my life changed on August 7, 1981, and then changed again not much more than twenty-three years later on February 18, 2005.

I describe the limits of my writing here partly to reflect my own feelings of inadequacy and frustration in coping with this matter. Not only do I have an incomplete memory and knowledge of the infinitely complex and intricate life of my son, but I also struggle to adequately understand what I do remember. While I write about many events and feelings in the pages that follow, in the end I still don't feel I have found any final comprehension of Graham's life or death. I can't possibly understand completely who Graham was, and I know I will never completely come to terms with his passing. Clarity is what I seek as I write, remember, and cry, but clarity remains elusive. Perhaps that is the nature of the situation, and to hope otherwise is either foolish or false.

Each person who came in contact with Graham in his twenty-three years of life has their own perspective—their own story to tell of this remarkable life and tragic death. Each friend, teacher, coach, and even casual acquaintance has a unique view of Graham. Even those who knew Graham best—his mother, three brothers, and me—will always have our own unique vision and memory of Graham. Such is the nature of loving someone with whom you have your own inimitable relationship.

And Graham was changing as he grew. As with every human life, his was a microevolution happening before our eyes. Carl Jung proposed that everyone is reborn three times in his or her lifetime. My Christian upbringing taught me about the virtue of being "born again," a spiritual rebirth that brought you closer to God. Then there are those who think each individual life has its own unique "trajectory" in which one grows in a constant continuum, transforming with time.

In my view, one is reborn many times during a lifetime, and Graham had already undergone several rebirths. His brothers noticed him changing, as did his friends. And though Mary and I could see him still struggling, we saw daily that an astonishing young man was emerging.

It is thus a heartbreaking but unavoidable exercise to speculate about who Graham might have become and how our relationships with him could have evolved. The awful finality of death is so difficult to deal with because it means the end of all possibilities. All dreams and hopes vanish in a single moment.

Graham's spirit continues to live within me. It expresses itself daily in one form or another. I think of him as I listen to music he enjoyed or perhaps would have later appreciated. Often, song lyrics seem to reflect an aspect of Graham's life or of my loss. I think of him often when I'm reading or watching a movie, traveling, walking through the deep woods or over mountain ridges—all activities he enjoyed. I think of him when I'm talking to people he knew. Even if they don't say anything about Graham, I can tell they are thinking of him and seeing the pain in my eyes. Some people are kind and brave enough to bring him up to me; others can't. But I think Graham is there in their thoughts nonetheless.

I believe Graham's spirit lives on in others. Some might think of him occasionally as they remember how he affected and enhanced their lives. Others will remember him each and every day and night. Like my mother, who frequently places her hand on a piece of paper tacked to her bedroom wall that bears a drawing of Graham's eleven-year-old hand. Graham traced his little hand when he visited his grandmother's Nebraska home in 1993. He drew a tiny star in the middle of his handprint and signed and dated it.

"Sometimes I just say, 'Hi, Graham,' and sometimes I say a little prayer," my mother told me once. "I say, 'I hope you are having a good time in heaven and I miss you and I love you.'"

And for me, Graham is always deep inside my being, and often foremost in my thoughts. When I hike in the mountains, I think of him. When I wake in the middle of the night, he is more often than not in my first conscious thought. Sometimes, when I dream, he revisits my world. I see him swimming in a lake with his brothers, all laughing, smiling, and playing. Sometimes we talk. Sometimes we hug. These are beautiful dreams.

It is difficult for me to portray Graham either accurately or completely. He was as complex a person as I have ever known—the opposite of simple or easy. He was unpredictable, clever, and self-aware. He was at times brazen and always fiercely independent, a characteristic he shared with his father. He was once an innocent, bright-eyed boy who loved life. He later became the rebel, sometimes with a cause and sometimes not. He made his own way through what often was a tormenting and frightening — and hopefully fascinating and beautiful — world for him. He practiced the philosophy of one of his favorite writers, Herman Hesse, who said truth is lived, not taught.

If there is an elegiac tone to my writing, please understand it is because that is the tone my life has taken. Without Graham, even my happiest times aren't as happy as they once were. His death has been and will continue to be a burden I bear, and that my family bears, as we live out our days and hopefully our years.

"Life is for the living," one of my aunts told me in the days after Graham died. I suppose I believe that is true, and I can see that focusing on the life that surrounds me may give me a measure of sanity and even happiness. But life also needs to include remembering those you knew, who were once such an intricate and powerful part of your life and who are no longer here. When I am gone, I want those who knew me, and especially those who loved me, to remember me for what I was and what I did. Not to mourn my death, but to simply remember my life, hopefully with some fondness and endearment.

I think that is perhaps what Graham would have wanted from me. So, I express my memory of him in the best way I know how: I write.

"If not now, then when? If not today, then why make your promises?"
— Tracy Chapman, *If Not Now*

chapter 1:

PROMISE

February 18, 2005, began beautifully.

It was another one of those perfectly clear Colorado mornings. The sky was a deep cerulean blue, as if fresh from an artist's brush, and the ponderosa pine trees that lined the park seemed to shimmer pure viridian green in the sunlight as I walked to my car. I had always enjoyed the colors of nature, but my painting class this morning had opened my eyes, and the world seemed particularly vivid and noticeable.

I had enrolled in the painting class just a month earlier, as part of my plan to pursue personal interests during a sabbatical. I had worked steadily over the years, first as a young journalist, and then for twenty years as a businessman with a bank owned by my wife's family. My two careers had been good to me, and I had enjoyed them. They had given me a means to be productive as well as a way to feed my growing family of four boys. But at the age of fifty, I found myself on January 1, 2005, in the fortunate position of taking a leave of absence from the workaday world. In the next few years, I would have the time to embark on a couple of new careers—newspaper columnist and art-gallery owner—until finding myself returning to the banking business in early 2009.

In February of 2005, life had never looked more promising. My wife and I were getting along better and were more in love than ever, after having been divorced for a couple of years and then remarrying in 2000. Together, we were designing the house of our dreams, to be built the following year on a beautiful piece of wooded land in the hills above Monument, with an expansive view of Pikes Peak. Our oldest son, Graham, had just enrolled for the first time in college at the age of twenty-three. After years of struggling to figure out what he wanted to do with his life, he had moved into a high-rise apartment in downtown Denver and had just begun classes at the University of Colorado–Denver. Our middle two sons, Will, twenty, and Seth, eighteen, were going to school at a smaller Denver college, where they both played basketball. And our youngest son, Colin, seventeen, was a junior in high school, keeping our house full of life and activity with his youthful personality and many companions.

Though we'd always been a close family, I was beginning to see our sons grow even closer as they became young men. I was enjoying watching their relationships mature.

As for myself, I was a healthy fifty-year-old, still able to run daily and frequently hike in the mountains. Free from the daily grind of my work at the office, I had ample time to do exactly what I wanted. Life could get no better than this, I thought.

The first thing I did with my new freedom was to enroll in an oil-painting class. I had loved art from a young age, drawing pictures of just about anything from as early as I can remember. On their basement wall, my parents still have my drawing of a Nebraska farm that won first place in a grade school art competition. Though my artist skills were mediocre, I had enough awareness of beauty to want to get it down on paper or canvas. And I continued to harbor the hope that, with a little time and training, I could be a real artist.

Unfortunately, like other parts of my life, this promise was soon to fade away.

The oil-painting class was offered by an art museum in downtown Colorado Springs, a half hour to the south of our home in Monument, a small community that sits high on the Palmer Divide between Denver and Colorado Springs. The art classrooms, with their paint-splattered and clay-stained floors, had a bohemian feel to them—quite different from my neat and tidy office back at the bank. I was pleased but a little uncomfortable with my change of venue. It felt a little wrong to be wearing a ball cap, sweatshirt, and jeans instead of the suit and tie I normally would wear on a workday. But there I sat, wide-eyed and alert on a wooden stool behind my easel, ready for instruction and artistic enlightenment.

Most of the other students in my class were women and older than me. They were primarily retirees as far as I could tell, done with raising their families and professional careers. Perhaps they were trying to reignite those artistic dreams they'd harbored when young and romantic, dreams that had been put off while they spent the prime of their adult lives working. That could have been said of me as well, although I was lucky enough to be a younger participant in the same cycle.

As I walked around the room looking at others' work, it was easy to tell who was going to be very good at this, and who was clueless. I was somewhere in between. The wide range of proficiencies in this small group puzzled me, and it made me admire the true masters—those who expressed profound beauty and meaning with a paintbrush, or any tool of art—more than ever.

I took to the painting fairly well at first, but I soon discovered it was more difficult to get it just right than I had imagined. It became increasingly frustrating that I couldn't translate the visions I had in my head onto canvas. It was like writing, where I often found that the wrong words came out first during those first drafts—or the right words in the wrong order—well before I could express what I really wanted. It was disappointing to see the paint I placed on the white canvas was the wrong color or the wrong shape. At the end of class, as I rinsed my brushes, I realized how discouraged I was with my progress. I had the sinking feeling that I was never going to succeed as a painter.

As I walked from the museum studios to my car, I soon forgot my artistic laments. It was a gorgeous Colorado morning, and this real world of color and shape was there simply to be enjoyed, not analyzed or captured on canvas. No matter how good a painter I was or wasn't, no matter how good I was at anything, it didn't take away from the pristine beauty of nature. A short walk through the park further cleared my head of self-doubt. I felt happy, reinvigorated. This was the real world. This was not discouraging to me.

Then my cell phone rang.

It was my brother-in-law Adam. "How is Graham doing?" he asked bluntly, without introduction or a preliminary greeting. His tone was serious, and I found the specificity of the inquiry odd. Adam and I were both family men, and we asked occasionally about each other's families, but in a general sort of way. It wasn't that we were disinterested or didn't care; we simply both lacked the ability to express freely our emotions or concerns about our families. Over our years of friendship, we seemed to have adopted a code of circumspection when it came to our most personal issues.

On the other hand, Adam was quick to size up problems, whether personal or professional, and address them head-on, with a few, direct words. If he considered something serious, then he was probably right.

"Not very well," I answered. "Why are you asking?"

I continued walking across the park to my car, but the bright colors of nature faded away to shades of grays. In fact, it was as if I suddenly saw nothing but the path below my feet as I walked with my head down. The world became an exchange of words on my cell phone, held tightly to my left ear. I tensed, my heart raced.

"Mom called this morning and said Graham called her last night, late, just to talk," Adam continued. "He said he wasn't feeling well. She was concerned about him."

These feelings of panic were not new to me. Graham had concerned me for some time—for years, maybe. I spent hours worrying about his well-being. Sometimes it seemed as if I spent more time worrying about him than not worrying about him. I often found my mood darkening in the middle of a situation in which I was happy and content, and more than likely it was because I had begun to worry about Graham.

Happy, energetic, and full of life as a young boy, Graham had taken a turn for the worse even before he entered his teens. When he was only nine years old, it became clear he was suffering from depression, and, over the years, we took him to a series of doctors who tried to assess and treat the illness. Graham underwent many hours of therapy, both individually and with us, his parents, and many changes in medication. But neither the therapy nor drugs seemed to help much.

As he entered his teens, Graham's mood deteriorated further. Although intelligent and well read, he struggled with the social and structural aspects of school. His grades began to tumble. He barely mustered enough credit hours to graduate his senior year. After high school, he avoided enrolling in or even thinking about college, working instead at our family's bank in Monument and then at one of our bank branches in Leadville, Colorado. He made a brief and ill-fated attempt to attend a community college in Colorado Springs, after we told him we would no longer support him financially unless he was a full-time student. Graham enrolled in some classes to appease us, but I don't think he ever showed up.

Finally, in January 2005, nearly five years after graduating from high school, Graham began classes at the University of Colorado–Denver, declaring a major in English literature. He moved into a high-rise building in the heart of downtown Denver, living alone in a small, one-bedroom apartment on the twenty-third floor. We were encouraged that, nearly five years after graduating from high school, he was putting his intelligence to some practical good and getting a higher education. Again, there was promise of change. Graham seemed to be getting his life together.

Despite my persistent worries, I was very pleased. It was going to be a good year.

"Are you alright? All of a sudden you went away. Are you alright?"
— Lucinda Williams, *Are You Alright?*

Chapter 2:

PHONE CALLS

On my cell phone in the park after my painting class, I told Adam we had seen Graham the night before, and he had been feeling sick. Our family had arranged to meet at the Rock Bottom Brewery in downtown Denver for dinner. Graham had arrived there some time before Mary and I. When we came in, he was drinking a glass of water, his face pale, drawn, and miserable. He said he thought he'd had the flu for a couple of days. Mary and I ordered beers and talked to him, waiting for his three younger brothers to arrive. Graham sat next to his mother, who put her arm around him. I sat across the table and felt grim, quietly watching Mary try to comfort her firstborn, as she had so many times before. I tried to talk Graham into coming home with us that night and sleeping at our house. I knew he had an appointment the next morning with his therapist in Colorado Springs and no classes in Denver the next day, because it was Friday. There was no reason to stay overnight in Denver, I tried to convince him. He could ride with his mother, and I would drive his car home. "Come home with us," I pleaded. "Come home with us."

But Graham insisted on staying in Denver. He said all he wanted was to walk the three blocks back to his apartment and go to sleep. He would come home the next morning and go to his doctor's appointment. Then he would stay at our house for the weekend, resting and recovering, so he'd be better for Monday morning and school.

It was a plausible enough plan, so we let him go. He tried to wait at the restaurant until his brothers arrived, but he finally said he felt so bad he needed to leave. We hugged him good-bye and he walked away, out the front door and past us on the Sixteenth Street Mall sidewalk, headed west toward his apartment. He glanced at me as he walked by the window, and I waved good-bye. He looked sick and sad. I had a sinking feeling, watching him walk away.

Then he was gone.

Just minutes later, Graham's brothers arrived. In contrast to Graham, they were excited and upbeat. The first thing they asked about was Graham, and we told them he was sick and had just left. They were disappointed to have missed him.

We always enjoyed getting together as a family. One of my friends once told me, "You sure are a close family. You seem to do everything together." I took that as a very pleasant compliment to our family, just the kind that made me beam with happiness. I was the most content when we were all together, and now that our three oldest sons had left home, those occasions were rarer. Our family get-togethers weren't always harmonious, but they were always filled with a wonderful energy. And maybe for the boys and Mary there were other feelings, but I always felt contented and complete when we were all together, if for no other reason than that we were in one place and I knew each of my sons was safe.

After dinner, the boys left, and Mary and I drove back to our home in the small town of Monument, an hour's drive south of downtown Denver. We'd made this drive to Denver and back many times to shop, dine, attend sporting events or concerts, and the like. Now that our three oldest lived in Denver, our trips were even more frequent.

The route south from Denver along the Front Range of the Rocky Mountains was one I knew well. By light of the moon or of the bright Colorado sun, the Front Range seemed to represent why Mary and I had come to this area a long time ago, and why we stayed. Punctuated by the fourteen-thousand-foot Pikes Peak to the south and the high mountains west of Denver, this first mountain range of the Rockies rises abruptly and beautifully from the plains, which spread to the east far toward our homelands of Nebraska and Kansas. It was the beginning of many mountain ranges that rise spectacularly to the west, which had fascinated and drawn me into their valleys and onto their peaks through many seasons.

Monument is perched on a sweeping high ridge, called the Palmer Divide, that rises over 7,000 feet above sea level between Denver and Colorado Springs. This small town, set in a wide swath of forested land, provided the perfect place to live and raise a family. This is the place to which Mary and I migrated in 1985 with our four-year-old Graham and our baby, Will, to set down our roots, and this is the where we intend to spend the rest of our days.

Driving along that graceful stretch of highway the night of February 17, 2005, I marveled at how the nearly full moon illuminated the mountains to my right, bringing out their sweeping silhouette. It was another beautiful, clear night along the Rocky Mountains.

Mary fell asleep as I drove, and I too was tired after the long day, dinner, and my concern over Graham. My cell phone rang, and it was Graham. Such calls from our sons were not unusual. After a visit they would often call to wish us a safe trip and to thank us for paying for the dinner or the activity we had just shared.

I didn't talk to Graham long; I was too tired. He asked where I was and how I was doing—the basic kind of courtesy Graham always showed me in our conversations. I asked how he was feeling. "Still not so good; but better, Pops," he replied weakly. He asked to talk to his mother, but I told him she was asleep. Our conversation lasted only a few minutes. We said goodnight. He told me he loved me, and I replied, "Love you too, Graham. Get some sleep."

I ended the call and put down the phone, driving on toward home in the dark.

Later, I concluded that Graham was reaching out to me with that call, and I didn't really understand or acknowledge it at the time. And it's very hard, because now every time I drive that road south from Denver, I remember the exact spot where I had my conversation with Graham. And I think about that conversation, and what it meant or didn't mean. Sometimes remembering that conversation on that particular stretch of highway makes me want to weep.

I'm convinced that spot on that road will haunt me forever.

After we got home, Mary and I quickly went to sleep. A short while later, our home phone rang. It was Graham. Mary picked up the phone as we both groggily woke ourselves. She sat up as she talked to Graham; I kept my head on my pillow, listening to Mary's words and straining to hear Graham's.

I could tell by Mary's tone that she was concerned, but not overly so. She told Graham that his speech was slurred. Had he taken too much of one of his medications? Graham said no, and Mary made him list the exact doses he'd taken. She seemed satisfied he had taken the correct dosages. They talked for some time, and I could hear Graham's voice coming out of the phone, but couldn't tell what he was saying. He didn't ask to talk to me, but that wasn't unusual. Eventually, Mary hung up the phone, and I asked how he was doing. Mary said she thought he was okay, but that she was worried about him. I fell back to sleep fairly quickly.

"Children are the great gamble. From the moment they are born, our helplessness increases. Instead of being ours to mould and shape after our best knowledge and endeavor, they are themselves. From their birth they are the centre of our lives, and the dangerous edge of existence."
— Josephine Hart, *Damage*

Chapter 3:

WINTER MORNING

The following morning, February 18, Mary and I got up and went about our business as usual without talking about Graham. He usually slept in, so there would be no checking on him until after his doctor's appointment at 11:00 a.m. I drove down to my painting class and enjoyed the session. Despite my newfound freedom from bank work, I was struggling to find interesting and inspiring pursuits to fill the void left by my three oldest boys who had left home.

Will, our second-oldest son, at this time in college in Denver, had been at the University of Redlands in the far-away Los Angeles basin the year before to study and play basketball. Suddenly, for the first time in our lives, we had a son living a thousand miles away. That had been emotionally difficult for Mary and me. After Will had left, I remember awaking one night to the sounds of Mary's sobs. She had turned on her nightstand lamp and held a picture of Will on her chest, staring at the photograph and crying. A mother's mother, I thought at the time. Her sadness was a harbinger of changes in our close-knit family as our children left home. It was inevitable and natural, of course, but it still was difficult to adapt after so many intense, pleasurable years living under the same roof.

Now, here I was, many winter mornings after bringing those baby boys home from the hospital, in a house devoid of the chatter and laughter of young boys, putting on a T-shirt and my paint-speckled jeans instead of a button-down shirt and dress pants, as I had for the past thirty years. I felt gloomy and unanchored, wondering why I wasn't enjoying my new freedoms as I thought I should. Without daily structure, I moved about tentatively, looking for something solid to attach myself to. For all its possibilities, being suddenly detached from the work I had done all these years, didn't feel comfortable. I worried about what my sons would think about a father who didn't go to the office every day. I felt like an inappropriate, nonproductive role model after years of being proud to represent the opposite. Though I was still technically employed and partially salaried, my ever-present worry about financially supporting my family increased.

But I had an even deeper concern.

Though Graham had made a big step in the right direction when he moved into his Denver apartment to attend school in January 2005, a recent crisis was fresh on our minds. In the summer of 2004, while he was living alone in his apartment in Colorado Springs, a friend warned us that Graham was experimenting with cocaine. We knew Graham used alcohol and marijuana, but this revelation shocked and alarmed us. I immediately scheduled a weekend trip to a cabin up by Estes Park for Graham and myself, and once we settled in, I confronted him with Karl's concern about his escalating drug use. At first he was angry and defensive, but the more we talked the more he acknowledged the danger he was putting himself into, and vowed to clean up his act and change his bad habits. It was at first a sad but then very hopeful time we spent together.

Mary and I did insist that Graham move back home with us. That summer, it seemed Graham had hit the bottom. He wearily but readily came home, as if he needed the time to recover and prepare to move on with his life.

When he moved out about half a year later, Mary and I were pleased with his decision. For years, I had gently pushed him to go to college. College had changed my life for the better, and I thought it could change his. After he finally decided to go to school, he seemed eager but anxious at the same time. Like a parent with a child going to kindergarten, I joined him on his first day of classes. We had lunch in the school's cafeteria-style restaurant, then sat outside in the warm January sunshine, watching kids—some his age, but most of them younger—walk into the building that housed his first class. Graham waited to go into the classroom until the last moment. He got up, said good-bye to me, and walked slowly through one of the doors. As it opened, I could see the large classroom full of noisy, talkative young men and women. Graham turned to me and gave me a grim look, and I smiled and waved. He disappeared into the schoolroom, much as he had when he was a four-year-old preschooler in Lincoln, Nebraska. And I had the same feeling as then: I was letting my son go into a world I could not control and which he would have to navigate on his own.

It was time. Graham was twenty-three.

Graham told me a couple of weeks later how traumatic those first days were. After his last class of the day, he would get in his car in the student parking lot, keep himself calm as he paid the parking-lot attendant, then cry. He sobbed in his car each day as he left school, he told me. For reasons I will never fully understand, going to school was a tremendous emotional burden for him.

I was thinking about these things as I walked to my car that morning on February 18, 2005. As I was appreciating the colors of a beautiful morning, I was also picturing Graham living in Denver by himself in the soaring downtown apartment building with its pale stone and black windows, terrified of school and dreading the next day. I was often preoccupied with this vision, a vision of my son's unhappiness, discomfort, and depression. This day was no different.

"Oh, where have you been my blue-eyed son? And where have you been my darling young one?"

– Bob Dylan, *A Hard Rain's a Gonna Fall*

Chapter 4:

NO ANSWER

My brother-in-law's phone call alarmed me more than usual. If he was concerned about Graham enough to call me, then did that mean something bad? I immediately called Graham's cell phone. There was no answer. I got his voice mail and left a message asking him to call me. Then I called our house and talked to Mary, asking if she had heard from Graham. She had not. Graham was supposed to be having an appointment with his therapist in Colorado Springs, but now I doubted Graham would have felt well enough to get out of bed and drive the hour or so from Denver to Colorado Springs.

I imagined him in his apartment, still asleep.

I drove from the center of Colorado Springs back to Monument, about a half-hour drive. I was anxious. I had been in this situation before with Graham. His sleeping habits had been unusual for years. He was often unable to sleep at night and would then sleep well into the day, sometimes even into the afternoon. And when Graham was finally asleep, it was very difficult to wake him. He had been this way since he was a baby: sleep was elusive when he wanted it, and completely captured him when it came.

So this was probably just another one of those times, I told myself as I drove north. The colors of the passing landscape, which had been so vivid just moments ago, now blurred and dulled with my emotions. Yes, of course, I reassured myself. This was just another one of those times. I had panicked many times before about Graham's well-being, only to find him sound asleep and safe in his own bed.

When I got home, I talked to Mary, who seemed less worried than I was, which reassured me. I continued calling Graham's number, but I hoped now that he was in his doctor's appointment and would have turned off his phone. The minute I knew the session was over, I began dialing his number. Slowly and carefully at first, faster and more panicked as time slipped on.

There was still no answer.

I decided to call the therapist, knowing I would get his answering machine. But at least he would call me back, perhaps after another session or several sessions. I left a message asking if Graham had attended his session, hung up, and waited. It wasn't too long before he called back. No, Graham hadn't appeared for his session. No, Graham hadn't called him.

Now I was feeling an extraordinary panic; one I'd never felt before, even after years as a fretful father. What if Graham was seriously unwell, unable to get out of bed? With all the medications he was taking, what if he lay unconscious? I tried to calm myself with the thought that Graham was deeply asleep in his bed in his Denver apartment. He would soon answer his phone when I called, or would see that I had been calling and call me back. Everything would be okay.

I kept calling.

It was now noon, and still no answer. I called Will, our second-oldest son, and asked if he had heard from Graham. He had not. Will lived with our third son, Seth, and a friend near the old Denver airport, several miles from Graham's downtown apartment. Will and Seth were attending a small college in that area, where they were studying business and playing basketball for the college team. Now that the three oldest boys were living as adults in the same city, they were growing closer, doing things together and seeing each other more frequently. They might have even talked to Graham that morning. They would know something that would alleviate my panic.

But in fact, they knew nothing of Graham's whereabouts this morning. They had no idea why Graham wasn't answering his phone. Just asleep, they agreed. Sick from the night before and sleeping and recovering, we conjectured together. We hung up and I continued to call Graham with the same result: nothing.

Now I had a decision to make. Somehow I needed to check on Graham. I called Will back and asked him to go check on Graham in his apartment. This was an ordeal, because Graham's apartment was a good half-hour drive away from Will and Seth's. Traffic could be bad in the center of Denver as well. I thought about driving up to Denver myself, but it was farther and would take longer. Will said he would go. Seth was in the shower, and so Will decided to go by himself.

I was fully panicked at this point, as was Mary. She sat near me in the kitchen, listening to every word I said on the phone and hearing my frantic tone.

Meanwhile, our youngest son, Colin, was home from school because he had final exams that day and finished early. In a conversation I can't remember we decided to have Colin go with Mary and me to Denver. As I look back, I can't say for sure why we made that decision. Was it a premonition that we all needed to be together? This part of our morning is foggy to me, because I was no longer thinking clearly. I can't even remember my state of mind, but it must have bordered on madness as I became unanchored from the normality and routine of the world and became fully anxious and singularly focused: where was my son, and why was he not answering his phone?

Regardless, the three of us piled quickly into Mary's car with Colin in the backseat trying to calm his parents, and headed north on the freeway to Denver. I remember pushing the car as fast as I thought safe, passing cars, warning myself not to do something stupid. My mind was rushing ahead, and I struggled to relax enough to drive. I can't remember what we said to each other. All I remember was talking almost constantly to Will on his cell phone, Mary and Colin listening in silence. Colin leaned forward from the backseat and placed his hand on Mary's shoulder. Mary lifted her hand and put it over Colin's.

A horrible scene was unfolding, and I could do nothing to stop it. It was as if we were being given time to brace for a fatal car crash, and the three of us were speeding to that nightmarish collision.

We were still on the highway when Will arrived at Graham's upper-floor apartment. When he knocked on the door, there was no answer. He knocked and yelled repeatedly, and there still was no answer. Nothing. Silence.

He went back down the elevator and to the main lobby of the apartment building, where the apartment manager's office was. The manager radioed a maintenance man to help Will get into Graham's apartment. Together, Will and the maintenance man somehow forced the door open. Will said later that as the door began to open, the man looked at him and told him to go first. Will entered the apartment and found Graham's body lying on the floor in the main room. His body was lifeless.

Like the place where I'd had that phone conversation with Graham the night before, I will never forget the exact spot on the road to Denver where Will called me and told me Graham was "gone." It was about a mile south of Castle Rock, not far from where I'd talked to Graham for the last time the night before. Will's words to me that morning will also forever be implanted deep in my soul. They are the worst words I have ever heard. They came from my poor second son, and they were something unbelievable about my first son. He said Graham was "gone" and then, as if to address my disbelief, he said, "Graham is dead."

I must have repeated the words verbatim—I can't remember for sure—because there was an immediate cry from Mary. I do remember she screamed, "Oh my God. No, no, no, no. Oh my God. My baby. Oh, my baby."

She was weeping and screaming at the same time.

I slowed the car so I could try to comfort her. I also slowed the car because speed was no longer the point. It was no longer necessary.

"Only love can leave such a mark. Only love can leave such a scar."
— U2, Magnificent

Chapter 5:

A KISS GOOD-BYE

When we arrived at Graham's apartment building, an ambulance and a police car were parked outside. The apartment manager, a young woman who had talked to Graham, Mary, and me a month or so earlier when Graham came to look at the apartment, greeted us. She was also the one who'd taken Graham's application, kindly helping him through the paperwork and making sure he was lined up to get the one-bedroom apartment he had wanted, high on the twenty-third floor. She walked out the front door of the apartment building with tears in her eyes, looking stunned and upset. She walked straight up to me and said something about feeling horrible that, while I had left her responsible for Graham's well-being, she had failed. I remembered I had joked with her after the application process was complete that I was handing over the responsibility for Graham to her. It was, of course, a well-intended attempt at humor, but I suppose at some level it revealed my deep concern about Graham, and now it carried a tragic irony. I could see it in her teary eyes that she genuinely felt she had let me down.

I hugged her and said of course I didn't hold her responsible for Graham, but she didn't seem convinced and slowly walked back to her office, where I could see her through the glass sitting at her desk, crying and watching our family.

The scene was a swirl of surreal movement, emotion, and conversation, all happening randomly and swiftly, although there was a dreadful slow-motion feeling to it all. Seth had joined Will at the building and the two of them were talking to a police officer when we arrived. Mary and I met our sons and embraced, and the EMT in charge of the ambulance service sat with us and briefly told us what he had found upstairs.

Soon, Will's girlfriend, Tara, came in the front door. We all sat on the couches in the lobby and talked and cried. The police officer asked if we wanted to go up to Graham's apartment, and Mary and I said we did. Colin, Seth, Will, and Tara stayed behind in the lobby. At this point, Will was the only family member who had been up to Graham's apartment.

Mary and I took a seemingly very slow elevator with the EMT, not talking to each other, our eyes straight ahead, watching each floor button light up as we were pulled upward. When we arrived at Graham's floor, we walked the short distance down the hall and through the doorway of his apartment. The door had been lifted out of its hinges and was leaning against the wall outside the apartment. When we entered Graham's apartment, we saw his body on a wheeled stretcher, about waist-high to me. His body was in a large, heavy, black bag, zipped to his chest. He looked asleep, expressionless. His beautiful eyes were closed, his long hair pulled back and away from his face. His skin was pallid, chalky. I remember thinking it was absolutely fucking unbelievable that I was standing there looking down upon my dead son. I didn't know what to think or feel. I didn't cry at first. Mary, standing at my side, was weeping quietly. I put my arm around her and pulled her close. We looked down together upon our firstborn baby, grown to become this tall, handsome young man, now lifeless before us. Nothing else existed in our world but this, this scene of death and disbelief.

A police officer stood in the doorway between the apartment's main room and the bedroom. He had looked at us as we entered Graham's apartment, mumbling something about being sorry. I said nothing back. I was at first puzzled and somewhat offended by his presence. I figured he had been summoned in case there had been foul play, or perhaps illegal drugs, involved in my son's death. I wanted him to leave, but he did not. He just stood there, silent. I suppose this was routine police procedure when responding to a 911 call and finding a young man dead in his apartment.

The EMT who had escorted us up to the apartment began to describe to Mary and me where they had found Graham's body on the floor in the main room of his apartment. Somehow, they'd calculated that Graham had died between midnight and early that morning. It was impossible to tell exactly when, he added. Mary and I stood there, listening to his words. We said nothing back to him. We asked no questions.

When he was done, we turned back to the stretcher where Graham's body lay. Mary and I said a few things to Graham. I wish I could remember what I said. I wish I could remember what Mary said. I cannot. Some memories will be with me forever, but they are locked away from my consciousness, kept deep inside as if to protect me from them. Some things I can't remember. Some things I don't want to remember.

I do remember standing next to my son and touching his cheek, feeling his soft skin with my fingertips. I do remember what that felt like. I then leaned slowly over and kissed his forehead. "Good-bye, Graham," I whispered to him. "I love you. I will love you forever."

Mary, tears dripping down her cheeks, also leaned down to say good-bye to her son. She kissed him on his cheek as I stood and watched. "My baby, my baby," she said.

I put my arm around Mary, her head hung as she sobbed, and we walked together out the open doorway.

> *"There's a hole in the world now. In the place where he was, there's now just nothing."*
> — Nicholas Wolterstorff, *Lament for a Son*

Chapter 6:
WONDERING

Mary and I returned to the lobby, where our three sons and Tara were waiting. We decided to leave Graham's apartment building and drive out to Will and Seth's apartment. Along the way, we called Graham's therapist and left a message on his answering machine that Graham was dead. It struck me as an odd message to leave on someone's machine. I can't imagine leaving a more important or serious message on anyone's machine. I supposed he had heard such things before. He'd probably had patients die before, and perhaps was used to it. I couldn't imagine getting used to this. The odd thing is that I don't think we ever heard back from him, or if we did, we missed it in the blurry days that followed. I was angry at this therapist for letting this happen, but also remembered that he had been of some help to Graham in the short time—maybe less than a year—that Graham had been going to him. I tried to let go of any anger or resentment I felt toward this man. It wouldn't bring my son back, and would only make me feel worse than I already did.

Graham had been going to therapists since he was young, probably as young as nine or ten years old. He first went to a psychiatrist in Denver. Usually, Mary would take him to his weekly visits, but occasionally I would drive him there and either wait in the lobby or go for a run from the office, which was situated alongside Cherry Creek in the middle of Denver. I would run along the creek's bike path toward downtown Denver. Imagining Graham's sadness and confusion as he sat in the doctor's stark office would make me want to cry. From time to time, Mary, Graham, and I would attend a family session at the doctor's office.

The general consensus was that Graham suffered from depression. Technically he was diagnosed with major depressive disorder (MDD). Thus began a seemingly endless attempt to find the right medication for him. Prescription after prescription seemed to offer him little relief. Each antidepressant's dosage was ramped up slowly, then ramped down when it failed to make way for the next ramp up. Nothing seemed to work well. It was Graham's misfortune to have a "treatment resistant" biological makeup. Then there was the talk therapy, which did seem to help to some extent. Graham battled the depression from early in his life right up to the fateful day of his death. The grip of this disease seemed to wax and wane, however, with some periods of relief.

Mary had suffered depression for most of her adult life, and her father, uncle, and siblings had at least some episodes of the disease. So it was no surprise that Graham was the recipient of genes that plagued him with the same tormenting biochemistry. Just before his death, yet another doctor put him on a very strong antidepressant that his mother had been on for years.

The drug Graham was taking, Parnate, was one of several in a group of drugs called "monoamine oxidase inhibitors" (MAOIs). The problem with MAOIs is that they can negatively interact with certain foods and over-the-counter drugs. These interactions can even send the body into what the medical world calls a "hypertensive crisis," which in turn can cause a heart attack. Because of their potentially lethal interactions, monoamine oxidase inhibitors have historically been reserved as the last line of treatment, used only when other classes of antidepressant drugs (for example, selective serotonin reuptake inhibitors and tricyclic antidepressants) have failed, as they had in Graham. Also for this reason, those using MAOIs are directed to wear a bracelet that says they are on this powerful, dangerous drug.

Graham did not have such identification.

Nor did he have a skin patch that was approved by the FDA to alleviate the risks of MAOIs interactions. The skin patch ensures that the drug does not enter the gastrointestinal system, thereby decreasing the dietary and drug interactions associated with taking the pills orally. Unfortunately, this skin patch wasn't on the market until February 2006, a year after Graham was gone.

As always with the disease of depression, it was difficult, if not impossible, for loved ones and doctors to tell if treatment was working. Sometimes it was hard to distinguish between behavior caused by the depression or the antidepressants and the "typical" behavior of the "real" patient. And I think that is why many people in our society don't even acknowledge depression as a disease, but rather mistake it for a personality trait, or worse, a character flaw.

It makes it even harder for those of us who haven't really suffered from the disease of depression to understand its effects on real sufferers like Graham. Of course, everyone gets down sometimes, and may even experience the deep mood swings we normally call depression. But this has nothing to do with the chronic, real disease of depression.

I have had only one brief bout of what might be called situational or marginal depression. There has been no history of depression in my family, at least not that I'm aware of. The only time I felt seriously depressed was in my second year of college, when it seemed the thrill of being young had worn off and I realized just how frightening and potentially meaningless life was. I was living with a fellow student whom I thought I liked and respected. It didn't take me long to realize how wrong I was. Maybe it wasn't him, but me, who changed. Either way, I became less fond not only of him but of his lifestyle.

For whatever reason, my life slowly but surely came down on me like a rain cloud getting darker and lower. Nothing excited or thrilled me. Life felt frightening, yet dull. Though I was never really suicidal, I failed to see the meaning or purpose in anything that I could see, touch, or hear around me. I continued to go to class and function at a level that kept me in college and moving ever so slightly forward, probably because I was so scared of flunking out and ending up working in construction, as I had during the summers between my school years.

It got bad enough that one particularly dismal Sunday afternoon, I walked from my apartment across the student athletic fields and into the front door of the student health center. I told them I wasn't feeling well and wanted to see someone about it. After waiting quite a while, I saw someone who might have been a doctor, but probably wasn't. He quickly and without emotion told me I was depressed, and gave me the phone number of the school's counseling center. I walked out the door and back to my apartment, feeling as gloomy as ever.

I did make an appointment a few days later with a pleasant young woman counselor and met with her a handful of times. With that little talk therapy and without resorting to medication, I began to feel better fairly quickly. I think I was simply fortunate enough to have depression-resistant genes. I'm sure if I'd been chronically depressed, I couldn't have regained my emotional center of gravity or adapted to the world around me so easily. And though my interior landscape is one of introverted melancholy borne of a very shy childhood, outwardly I am fortunate to have acquired enough social skills to behave in a way that most see me as a stable, happy, and even-tempered middle-aged man. In other words, I consider myself one of the lucky ones.

Studies show that, although all human beings are subject to misfortune, the brains of some people don't recover as quickly as others. These are the people who get depressed and stay depressed. There are parts of the brain—mostly the hippocampus—that regulate one's sense of well-being and happiness, which can become so damaged with either repeated disappointments or a single trauma that they cannot recover on their own to a normally functioning state.

I will remain forever frustrated that I could never really understand the depth and true nature of Graham's emotional distress, even though I knew how real and terrible it seemed. He constantly talked about the meaninglessness of the world around him and his own inability to make sense of it or to simply feel happy. There was sleeplessness, nightmares, self-doubt, torment, and at times anger. The doctors can call it a mood disorder, and the books can describe at length what they think is going wrong with a depressed person's brain chemistry, but neither comes close to describing the full power of this ugly disease over my son.

It had affected my son on so many of his anxious days and restless nights, and now I was faced with the possibility that it had taken his life. The former I had reluctantly come to terms with over the years, the latter I could not.

"Where is that child of mine tonight?"
– Kiki Dee and Carmelo Luggeri, *Under the Night Sky*

Chapter 7:

DUSK

After leaving that awkward message for Graham's therapist, we drove farther east on the freeway toward Will and Seth's apartment. Colin was in the backseat. I was driving, with Mary beside me in the passenger's seat. Will and Seth followed us in their cars. I was in a daze, not knowing what to think or feel. It was sunny outside, and the freeway was busy with midday traffic. Cars were everywhere, speeding to the west and the east, and it seemed that our bleak little caravan was just another piece of some giant, uncaring human flow. As I caught glimpses of the faces in the cars that passed us, I detected a simple, striking sadness in each of their expressions. It wasn't just me who was sad; everyone seemed sad that day.

This was my new world.

Soon after we got to Will and Seth's apartment, Graham's best friend, Karl, came over, and then Mary's brother Adam arrived. We shared how this tragedy had unfolded for each of us. At some point during this dreadfully surreal afternoon, Will found a crumpled piece of paper in his trashcan. It was a short essay that Graham had written for a class just the week before. Graham had come over to print the essay because his own printer was broken. He had thrown one of the copies into Will's trashcan. We smoothed the paper, and, incapable of reading it aloud, passed it around and read it silently, one by one. When it was my turn, my hands trembled as I held the paper. I read it through teary eyes. It read:

Defining Myself

I would like to consider myself a man of many faces, much like Hesse's infamous Steppenwolf. *I am fundamentally a sad and lonely person, but I do possess a sense of humor and enjoy relaxing and hanging out with friends every so often. I probably take myself and the world around me too seriously. I am very sensitive and analyze every event in my life to the fullest extent. You would think this would make me quite industrious, but that is quite to the contrary. I am probably the laziest and most slothful man alive. I despise school and work. I just don't carry it in me to be told what to do. Even working on this essay now, which is on a very simple topic, I feel bad. I am obsessed by the macabre and can't tolerate bright lights or direct sunlight.*

But every once in a while, I'll feel a surge of happiness and contentment equal to ten dark nights of misery. I adore the arts, especially music, and am very fond of animals. Often only these two things can dull my pain. I also love to travel. Traveling is a great way to escape. I also have a great passion for the night sky, which I gravely miss after my recent move to smog-infested Denver. Speaking of moving, I have shifted residences at least four or five times since the age of eighteen, restless in my journey to find contentment. I have been from Buena Vista out by the Collegiate Peaks to Colorado Springs (a few different places there), and then, most recently, up to the city of Denver.

I enjoyed a great childhood. I have great parents. They have always been very supportive of me, even through my times of great sloth and deep depression. They don't really understand me but I know they try. I was born in Omaha, Nebraska, moved shortly after to Lincoln, then spent the next couple of years there. My father was then offered a job in Colorado Springs. We built a great house, which I lived [in] from age five to eighteen. I love that house. It defines many, many years of my life.

I have never liked school (as you can tell by my five-year break from high school to college). I always tested well and was even offered to move up a grade. I was always in advanced classes with the older kids, but didn't do my homework (partly due to a quite severe drug habit) and got mostly Cs and Ds the latter half of high school. I just never liked being told what and when to do it. I wished for a system in which the teacher would tell us what material we would be tested on [and] then be tested on it. I always wondered about the validity of homework, anyway. Is it just practice for the test, or [is] it just to keep us busy and out of trouble at a "vulnerable" age? And the teachers never do any work. They always just say "read this" or "read that." Why wouldn't they ever teach us the material themselves? Very few teachers have taught me anything directly themselves. There is the exception of a couple of math and history classes. Teachers are bad. Education is good.

Part of the reason I didn't exactly excel in high school was that I was distracted by music. I play both the guitar and, to a lesser ability, the piano. I own over five hundred CDs, not counting tapes and vinyl. This consumed much of my time, as I was constantly writing music or playing with bands. This was also a great relief from my depression, maybe because I was writing the most depressing music in the world. I also considered myself a member of the counterculture, a rebel. I would smoke pot until daylight, listening to Pink Floyd and reading novels. I was useless. I shouldn't say "was," because I still am, of course.

It is easy for me to find things that make me feel suicidal, but it is quite another to find things that ease my mind. One of those things, of course, is music. Without music, I wouldn't be here writing this paper. Both the creation, and lately especially, the listening of music bring great soothing to my mind. Also, the seeking of new music is great. And I couldn't do without a good concert a month. Another thing is animals. My parents own two dogs and a cat, with whom I grew up. They are such innocent creatures, and can sense when I am feeling rotten. They cannot judge you or speak ill of you. They can just love. I also get a huge kick out of being in nature. I love to camp, preferably by myself, but with a good friend is just as good sometimes. It is just so relaxing and real out there in the great, majestic, forested mountains. Nothing but you and the air, so pure. I do this year round. If I couldn't, I would be driven mad.

I am a very negative person, when it comes down to it. Everything is a downer. But there are things that keep me going. The love of my family…I have three very cool brothers…music, books…somehow I have neglected to talk about their huge impact on my life in this essay, the love of my animals, and nature. I lead a life of misery but sometimes I think it just makes me stronger.

Despite the slight optimism in his essay, Graham clearly was still struggling with his depression and with school. After we all had read Graham's essay, we talked about whether Graham might have killed himself, or if this had been an accident.

"Honestly, the whole school thing was not a good fit for him," Karl said. "It stressed him out a lot…He didn't want someone else to tell him what to do. His learning process was different. He wanted to be on his own level. He wanted to be self-taught, like how he learned music and philosophy. Maybe he should have been taking upper-level courses, if he was going to go to school at all. He was very anxious and had a hard time sleeping over the whole school thing."

Karl said Graham never talked about being depressed and never once mentioned wanting to take his own life. And they talked about a lot of things over the many years they knew each other. They'd lived together for a year in a Colorado Springs house, and they'd seen each other regularly since Graham had moved a month earlier to Denver, where Karl already was living and studying music and philosophy at the University of Colorado-Denver.

"I honestly think it was a complete accident, what happened to Graham," Karl said. Everyone agreed Graham wrote with too much optimism in his essay for it to be a premonition of suicide. Everyone agreed, that is, but me. Graham had talked to me about not wanting to be alive; had said that being gone from this life was the only way he was going to get relief from his own internal anxieties and unhappiness.

This question would haunt me for months to come.

Our cell phones kept ringing. One by one, we'd leave the room to take calls from friends and family members. I remember most clearly talking to one of my closest cousins, a year younger than me, who had lost his father to alcoholism very early, and to a friend whose son had almost died of a brain tumor. A couple of times, someone would be overcome by emotion and leave the main room. One or all of us would join that person and try to comfort them, or at least try to embrace them and be there, for there was no real way to comfort them. We would huddle in a darkened bedroom, hugging each other and sobbing.

As the day slowly turned to dusk, fatigue set in, and my memory became unclear. It was as if my brain, overwhelmed by emotion and trauma, began to shut down. Somehow we found a place to eat and then all drove back to Monument, where the day had begun for me in a very different way than it had ended. I'm not sure how we suffered through the night, the worst we had ever shared. I don't think Mary slept much, and I drifted in and out of sleep. We talked off and on through the night, huddled in the bedroom we had shared for so many years, with its large windows framing the beautiful Rocky Mountains to the west. These were the mountains I had so enjoyed and shared with Graham. These were the mountains we both loved. Now, faintly visible in the moonlit night, they seemed meaningless and pointless.

Sadness covered both of us like some awful, suffocating blanket. There was no escaping our feelings. I imagined at one point that someone might call us and tell us that we had been wrong, that Graham was not gone, that the worst thing that could happen to us hadn't really happened that day.

But that phone call did not come. The worst thing had happened to Mary and me that day. We had lost our baby, our Grahamie. He was gone.

"They tell me everything is going to be alright, but I don't know what alright even means."
— Bob Dylan, *Tryin' to Get to Heaven*

Chapter 8:

DAYBREAK

The next few days were a blur. It was as if the very essence of who I was, particularly that part of me who took such refuge, peace, and happiness in being a father, was rejecting reality, erasing memories as they happened. My self-awareness was shielding itself from the pain of having just lost my son.

A strange numbness replaced my normal awareness of the world around and within me. In retrospect, I suppose these feelings were the body and mind's natural defenses kicking in against this raw, unbearable, unthinkable event.

Suddenly and irrevocably, the thing I feared and dreaded the most was full force upon me. I, of course, like any other parent confronted with this kind of situation, was not prepared.

I had the sense the news of Graham's death spread quickly in the community where we had lived for twenty years, passing from household to household in phone conversations or in spontaneous gatherings in grocery store aisles. I knew this was happening, because very quickly we began receiving phone calls and cards in the mail. Some of the bravest would actually stop by the house, walking up our long driveway to our front door. And though it was as difficult a door for our family to answer as well, these visits were oddly helpful. I remember standing in the entryway of our home, hugging friends awkwardly, neither of us knowing what to say to each other. Still, it meant something that these friends came to see us and showed they cared about our family.

It was interesting to me that people brought gifts with them, often food, but sometimes symbolic offerings of sorts. One friend of Graham's brought a bottle of Navan, a French cognac. He told us that it had been a favorite of Graham's that the two of them had once enjoyed together. Like so many others, he came into our home, grim-faced and apologetic, saying what he could muster, and leaving as quickly as he could. As we closed the door behind this friend of Graham's, Mary and I were left alone together, standing in the entryway. Mary clutched the bottle of cognac tightly to her chest, as if it were some precious trophy she had just been presented. In silence, we embraced, as we would many times in the days to come, and Mary sobbed, her tears falling onto my shirt. "I don't understand," she said. "I just don't understand. I have all these feelings, and I can't do anything about them. I'm so angry and confused and sad. I'm so, so sad. Where is my Graham? Where is my baby? I want him back."

I took the bottle from her as she stood there, her tear-filled eyes desperately seeking answers I couldn't give her. I walked into the kitchen to put the bottle in our liquor cabinet, among the few other mostly full bottles that Mary and I rarely took out of the cabinet. Before placing the bottle in the cabinet, I stopped to admire the bottle of Navan, a "vanille noire naturelle de Madagascar." I scanned the label. "A spirited experience crossing all boundaries. Embrace," it read.

I pictured Graham sitting with his friend, sipping the cognac and "spiritedly" talking about philosophy, literature, or music; crossing many boundaries, embracing the life within him and around him. And now he was gone, never to sip this or any other cognac again, never to embrace his friend, or his father for that matter, again.

I remember thinking in those first few days how utterly difficult it must have been for people to come to our house to see us. They would have had to make a conscious decision to visit our family, driving through our rural neighborhood to our tiny, quiet cul-de-sac. Cars were in the driveway already, night and day, so these visitors most likely would have had to park on the street and walk up our steep, lengthy drive, finding themselves in front of a windowless, red wooden door. They must have felt strong anxiety or sadness, or both, as they did so.

I would have then. Now, when I visit families who have lost a loved one, I have a strange calmness about it all, as if the fear and the anxiety has been vacuumed from me.

They would not have known who was going to answer the knock at the door. Perhaps it would be the father of the son who had just died, or perhaps the sobbing mother, maybe one of the brothers. I admired those who came to visit for their courage, and will long remember each and every one of them.

Many people came. Friends of Mary's, people from my office, friends of the boys. Most people visited only briefly, but others wanted to come into the house and sit and talk to us at length. I always hoped for the quicker visit, just because it was uncomfortable and tiring to talk to them at any length. Sometimes Mary couldn't handle the people coming and would stay in her bedroom. I felt an obligation to be downstairs, and sensed that it was somehow easier for me than for Mary, although many of the people who came were more interested in seeing Mary than me. I stopped drinking any alcohol during this period, and I'm not sure why. I would tell people that I wasn't sure I would ever stop drinking if I started, but that wasn't really the reason. I think I felt I needed to be there for my family, sober, aware, and able to help them as I could. The last thing my family deserved was for me to leave them emotionally. In this time more than any other, they needed all of me, no matter how unequal to the situation I might have felt. And conversely, they were there for me. I don't know what I would have done if they hadn't been.

On the morning after Graham's death, I fetched the newspapers. It was such a constant in my life, this short morning walk to the end of the driveway to bend over and gather up a couple of newspapers in plastic wrappers. I always enjoyed the fresh morning air hitting my skin and lungs as I moved and breathed.

The sameness of this routine felt like a dream the day after my son died, as if I were floating as I walked down the driveway. It was as if I were so overwhelmed by a new, shocking emotion that I was somehow detached from the external world. At the same time, ironically, I felt very alive. Maybe this was caused by my stark sense of a contrast between my aliveness and Graham's death. My senses were acutely aware and alert. I registered the blackness of the driveway under my feet, the greenness of the ponderosa pine trees that the driveway cut through, and the blueness of the sky. It was all so real and vivid. I remember being puzzled by this feeling of being so alive, when I expected to feel numb, blurred, and deadened.

This was the day I first experienced a pattern of emotion that would repeat itself often in the days, months, and years to come. These feelings were deeper than any I'd ever experienced. First came an overwhelming sense of sadness, followed by a strange calmness and disconnect from the world around me. Not being a religious, spiritual, or mystical person, I normally look to logic and facts to explain what I felt. But now, faced with this singular loss, I was unable to comprehend what my body—soul, if you wish—was going through. Maybe this was my "soul" coping with the loss in the only way it knew how. Maybe it was an effort to continue to connect to Graham. Maybe the calm I felt after deep sadness was nature's way of helping me avoid insanity. Whatever the cause, this often-repeated cycle of sadness and calm has become the core of my grief.

My emotions were a weather pattern, an icy wind in the dark of night, followed by a quiet stillness as the storm passed and the silent stars began to sparkle in the night sky.

"Sorrow is no longer the island but the sea."
— Nicholas Wolterstorff, *Lament for a Son*

Chapter 9:
FATHERS AND SONS

Our extended families began to arrive fairly quickly, most coming from Kansas and Nebraska, where Mary and I grew up, respectively. Everyone was helpful and thoughtful, but as I ran into family around the house, there was a strange, underlying, un-discussed awareness of the whole dreadful reason we were together in the same house. This was the worst kind of reason for being together, and everyone knew it. Graham was gone, and it was as if our families rushed in to fill the void. As much as I'm sure they wanted to, they couldn't.

Graham's death was like an invisible cloud that permeated each room and hallway of our home. It was impossible to escape. Mary's dad and my dad seemed to team up and got busy cleaning up the outside of the house, partly because they needed something to do, and partly because they wanted the house to look nice for visitors. I wonder now what they might have said to each other, each having lost their first grandson, each feeling sad and confused but probably unable to express it to each other.

Maybe they did talk about it. I walked outside at one point during the day, and they were picking up cigarette butts that Graham had tossed into the trees from the front porch. They were putting them in small plastic grocery bags marked "thank you." I stood there on the front porch watching this scene unfold, trying to comprehend its significance. Here was Mary's father picking up the remnants of the very things he hated (his mother smoked her entire life and died eventually of emphysema). What a bitter feeling he must have been experiencing. Then there was my father, stooping to pick up the butts, a man who had smoked cigarettes since he was a sixteen-year-old farm boy and didn't give up until he was in his 80s. Then there were the contrasting sizes of these men. My father was slight and short, less than six feet tall. Mary's father was the opposite in almost every way: large, tall, and broad. But there they were, together in my front yard, brought together years ago by the marriage of their children and now by their grandson's early death.

As I stood on that front porch, I remembered waking especially early one morning just weeks before Graham's death. I'd come down from our bedroom on the upper floor to make a pot of coffee in the kitchen. Opening the front door to fetch the newspapers, I was surprised to see Graham sitting alone in the predawn dark on a porch step. He puffed on a cigarette, its orange tip glowing brighter as he inhaled. He turned to me and said, "Hello, Pops." I sat down with him and we chatted, me groggy from sleep and he anxiously alert from sleeplessness.

This was his nighttime spot when he couldn't sleep, which was often, he told me. Since we had no streetlights, he could take in the full dark of the woods in which we lived, with its canopy of sparkling night sky. This is where he came when he was awakened by a bad dream or by his medicine interrupting his brain's chemistry. After tossing and turning in the childhood bed he had recently returned to after living alone in a Colorado Springs apartment, Graham had little choice but to pull himself from the warmth of his covers and shuffle outside to sit on the porch. Graham had always said he enjoyed being outside at night, but as far as I could tell these solitude sessions were not about enjoyment, but rather restlessness, sleeplessness, and depression.

Now, standing on the porch in the daylight the day after Graham left us, I could only imagine what he'd thought or felt there in the silent, cold night, the only light coming from his cigarette and the stars above. Was he worried, concerned, frightened, or angry? Was he relaxed and enjoying the respite from his daytime stress and nighttime bad dreams? He often told me of both. Now, standing there, my own mind messed up and far away, I only knew I could no longer ask Graham himself.

The guests kept coming, passing over the step where Graham had sat. They came loaded down with armfuls of food and drink, offering hugs, tears, and comforting words. These guests did and said what they could to somehow make us feel better about something we couldn't possibly feel better about. The support did help, in that I knew these people really cared about our family—those of us still around. It helped to hear them say kind things about Graham, reminding us what a unique and wonderful person he was and what he had added to the lives of those he had come into contact with over the brief span of his twenty-three years.

One of those first mornings, my father and I sat in our dining room together trying to find words of comfort for each other. Not normally expressive men, both of us stammered out words that didn't seem to really relay how we felt. My father's eyes filled with tears as he looked into mine. "I just wish it could have been me instead of Graham," he said. "I'm an old man. He was not."

We began almost immediately to prepare for a memorial service for Graham, which offered the distraction of specific, concrete details. I remember Mary's oldest brother, Wint, sitting down with us in the kitchen to talk to us about Graham and his life so that he could put together a eulogy. We talked for quite a while about Graham's life, who he was, and what made him special. Wint, a lawyer, wrote all of it down on his yellow legal pad.

People were walking around our house, providing a strange, quiet kind of commotion as a backdrop for our conversation. There were my sisters from Lincoln and their families. There were Mary's siblings, most from Kansas, and some of their families. There were aunts, uncles, and my elderly maternal grandmother, Kaja. Never before had such a collection of relatives assembled in our house at the same time. There were the close friends of my three youngest sons. And, occasionally, friends of Mary's and friends of mine came to our somber home, talked with us, and left.

As our conversation with Wint ended, I told him that I didn't want to put Graham on a shelf to be forgotten. I remember saying this with a surprising amount of confidence and strength, as if I had been through this before or knew what I was saying. I didn't know what I was saying. I didn't know what that meant. I really had no idea what I was talking about.

Wint readily wrote down my wish, however. It was something he would recount with the same kind of commitment a couple days later at the memorial service.

Now, years later, I still don't really know what my wish meant. Having read countless books on grieving and recovery, I have a better understanding of how one survives and slowly heals after the trauma of losing a loved one. But there is no forgetting, no wiping the slate clean and starting over. Even if you wanted to, you couldn't "put on the shelf" the person you can't live without, but have to. It would not be possible. It would not be real.

I read some succinct if misguided advice in one book on grieving: "Believe it, bear it, bury it." I'm not sure if any one of those three goals is achievable for any parent who has lost a child. At least for this father, I'm not sure I'll ever believe or bear what happened to me, and I certainly won't be able to ever fully bury my son.

"Oh brother I can't, I can't get through to you. I've been trying hard to reach you 'cause I don't know what to do. Oh brother I can't believe it's true. I'm so scared about the future and I wanna talk to you."

– Coldplay, *Talk*

Chapter 10:
BROTHER

I struggled immediately, and still do, in talking to Mary and my sons about Graham's death. It is not like putting Graham on a shelf, because I think about him and feel for him each day. But perhaps it's been easier to put him on my own internal shelf, so I don't have to go through the painful process of sharing what I'm feeling. In a way, I can't fully share what I'm thinking about Graham or what it feels like to have him gone, so any effort to do so becomes frustratingly incomplete.

I have felt bad many times about not being able to fully support either Mary or the boys. Mary is more assertive about asking for support, and I can offer up a hug or some words of comfort—but, again, I feel I have not done enough. I essentially spend much of my time avoiding talking about Graham with Mary, and that disappoints her. I don't avoid listening to her, and this is helpful to me and hopefully to her. Often, she will say something I am already feeling, or she puts her feelings out there in a way that clarifies my own.

With my sons, it's different. Like me, they tend not to bring it up. There are times I feel I should take the lead as their father and ask how they're doing or what they're feeling. Obviously there are things deep inside them that are weighing on them, churning and causing them sorrow and confusion. But it is only occasionally that we speak about our sadness over Graham.

I remember an encounter with my son Colin during the summer after Graham died. Mary's family had met for a family reunion on Vancouver Island. We were all gathered for drinks and food in the resort's big room. It was dusk, and the room overlooked the beautiful, gray-and-blue sea curling in between the numerous islands. I went to the window and looked at the scene, sad and beautiful at the same time. In the darkening sky above was the moon, beginning its descent to the western horizon.

As it always did, the moon reminded me of Graham, as if he were shining his mellow, grey-white light down on my teary eyes. Colin came up behind me and put his arm around me. I said, "Look at the moon, Colin. Isn't it beautiful?"

He turned his head and looked directly into my eyes. "I know, Dad, I know."

That kind of connection between a grieving father and a bereft brother might not be a textbook disclosure of feelings about loss, but it means the world to me. And as Colin told me years later, when I asked him if he ever talked to his friends about Graham, "No one's in your world. No one understands really how you are feeling." Only our family knows what it's like to have Graham gone.

In as few words as possible, because words can get in the way and confuse the already confused, we acknowledged from one soul to another that we had the same feelings about the same person. I have had similar exchanges with my other two sons and with Mary. And though those deep emotions might not be voiced, they will always be felt individually and collectively, and we will always know it.

Seth started opening up years later about his brother. One day in my office (Seth now works with me), he began a long monologue about seeing Graham two nights before his death. Graham came over to Seth and Will's apartment. Graham was in a particularly good mood, and the three of them played music and talked. Seth was lip-synching the music and dancing, something he did often to entertain his brothers, and he said Graham was cracking up at the scene. I'd witnessed this before and Graham would begin a huge belly laugh at Seth's antics, insisting Seth keep the show going. And Seth would.

Seth and Graham hadn't always had a great relationship. They were both stubborn young boys with strong personalities, and the older brother wasn't always very pleasant with his younger brother. But that, fortunately, had been changing.

"I was really just getting to know Graham," Seth said. "I'd grown up thinking he was so much older and so much smarter. Like he was over my head. But that was just beginning to change when I got to college. Graham treated me differently, too, more as an equal."

Now Seth and his brothers are left to wonder what happened to their brother. If it is difficult for an adult who has lived longer and experienced more death to understand these things, how much more difficult must it be for them, who were so young when Graham died?

"Graham was a hundred percent there one day and zero percent there the next," Will once told me as we sat around a campfire. "I don't know what happened to him."

Maybe to help bring the memory of his brother to life, maybe just to honor him, Will and Tara would make a dramatic choice on January 2, 2011, to name their son after Graham. The Nooney and Stingley families were all gathered in a small waiting room of St. Joseph Hospital in uptown Denver, when Will appeared to announce the birth of his first-born. I'll never forget him saying the words: Walden Graham Stingley. Maybe it wasn't the name so much as the fact that there was a new life brought into this world by my own son and the beautiful mother of this healthy little baby, Tara, who had been so disciplined during pregnancy and worked so hard to naturally birth her baby.

But the name meant something. It was the bringing together of the past and the future. It symbolized love for what had been and hope for what could be. And when Will and Tara asked me what they wanted Walden Graham to call me I did not hesitate. "Pops," I said. "I want him to call me Pops."

"Give me a word, give me a sign, show me where to look, tell me what will I find, oh, heaven let your light shine down."
— Collective Soul, *Shine*

Chapter 11:
MUSIC IN THE CHAPEL

The memorial service itself was sad, yet somehow beautiful. We weren't a church-going family, so immediately we had a logistical problem about where to hold a service for Graham. We had attended the All Souls Unitarian Church in downtown Colorado Springs when the boys were younger, but eventually the pastor we liked so much moved away to another church, and we stopped going. Mary and I had gone a few times to a new Unitarian church closer to our home, but we couldn't get into a regular Sunday routine, although we did like the pastor there, a young man named Matthew Johnson-Doyle. We decided to ask him to conduct Graham's service, but his congregation was meeting in a temporary location, so he had no place to conduct the service. After considering several possibilities, we settled on Shove Memorial Chapel, a beautiful, Norman Romanesque cathedral built nearly eighty years earlier in the campus center of The Colorado College, just a block from downtown Colorado Springs. I'd been there just once, for a ceremony conducted by Buddhist monks, and fell in love with the chapel. Raised in a church-going family, I retained a love of churches as I grew older, even though I outgrew attending them. As a tourist in various cities, one of my favorite things to do is visit churches and cathedrals, both the quaint and small and the spectacular and grand. I've always been fascinated, even slightly mesmerized, by the buildings themselves and the unique feeling they inspire, making me feel like nothing else could as I would open their front doors and walk into their sacred spaciousness.

Shove Chapel was not only a special place architecturally, with its light brownstone exterior, its soaring interior, and its intricate, dark, wood-beamed ceiling, but it also had the right feel for Graham's service. It was a serious and spiritual place that was tolerant of all religious or philosophical views. Despite its traditional cruciform design and traditional Christian architecture, it contained a wide variety of artistic and architectural symbols. Above the huge organ pipes at the front of the chancel, for example, was a very unusual ten-petal rose window instead of the traditional cross. The ten petals symbolized the fundamental disciplines of liberal education. And in addition to several portraits of Christ, there were depictions of great teachers in the humanities and science, such as Galileo and Charles Darwin. Graham would have liked this place, perhaps particularly the medieval feel it had.

The morning of the service, Mary, the boys, and I crowded silently into one car and drove the half-hour from our home in Monument to the church. No one talked. We were unsure of what to say and still stunned by what had happened to Graham. I remember arriving at the parking lot near Shove Chapel and walking together across the lawn of the campus to the front door of the chapel. One of the managers from our bank had backed his pickup up to the front door and was unloading wooden easels into the narthex of the church, which would hold pictures of Graham and our family.

When you entered the church, the most immediate feeling was one of darkness and heaviness. It wasn't until you walked into the main part of the church, where the ceiling lifted dramatically, that the darkness lifted and the space felt solemn but peaceful.

Graham's closest friend, Karl Deiotte, was busy connecting a music CD he had made for the service to the chapel's sound system. Together with Will, he had chosen a compilation of songs that had meant something to Graham or those closest to him. The music swirled around the grandiose space of the church as people started showing up. They entered the chapel through large front doors and immediately saw the four easels of pictures. Mary's dear friend, Debbie Ross, and Tara had painstakingly chosen these photos out of literally hundreds. Working in our basement, Tara and Debbie then glued each of the pictures on the posters during the few evenings preceding the service. This beautifully crafted collage of Graham's life, from his baby years on, was very painful for me to look at, and I did so only briefly. For several years after the service, those posters remained downstairs in our storage room, covered by the same black plastic someone had wrapped them in for their trip to our house from the chapel.

People slowly filled the chapel. Besides family, there were many friends, both of Graham and our family. It was strange and awkward, but good, that so many people whom we had known in one way or another during all our years in our small Colorado town would come to the service. I didn't want this attention, but felt supported by it nonetheless. I'd been to a few other funerals and memorial services for people who had died unexpectedly, a few for children who had died, and remembered feeling sick and awful for those who were at the center of this attention. It is all well meaning, of course, but so terrible at the same time.

I couldn't help but imagine what Graham would be thinking about his own service. He was as uncomfortable with attention as I was, certainly more than the average person. He might have even been cynical or angry about the attention, as he was about most conventional human behavior. Maybe he would have been flattered by it. I think he grew up hungry for attention in many ways, the oldest of four boys who were born rather close together, from his birth in 1981 to Colin's in 1987. It was a full household with strong, bright, curious, and capable personalities, and it must have been difficult for our sons to feel as if they got enough attention in the family. Fortunately, there was a lot of love between the boys. You only have to look at the picture of a six-year-old Graham proudly holding his newborn baby brother, Seth, to see his pure joy, happiness, and love.

I can't really know for sure what it was like for the four brothers to vie for attention as they grew up in the same home. It contrasted with my own childhood; I was an only son born in between two sisters, one three years older and the other six years younger than me. It was all too easy for me to get attention in my family, and I think it has benefited me throughout my life. Despite my own, very different childhood, Mary and I were fully aware of this delicate situation and tried to treat each of our sons fairly and independently, dealing with each as an individual and not as one of the group. But it was impossible to give them all the attention they really wanted or needed. There were things to do before bedtime, places to go before game time, and of course, the sheer fatigue that got in the way of perfection. And as the babies kept coming, Graham, I think, often got the shorter stick of the family tree. With younger offspring to care for, we assumed Graham could fend for himself. It was Graham whom we always perceived as older and therefore more capable.

Now, in the cathedral-sized room, Graham was finally getting the full attention of his family. And it was too late.

I also wondered, with some discomfort, what Graham would have thought about the setting of his service. After all, this was his life we were honoring, and I wanted to be true to him. Given Graham's discomfort with and mistrust of organized religion of any kind, would it have bothered him? The Shove Chapel certainly had the look and feel of a sacred place, a place of the spiritual - the mystical - that may have intrigued Graham.

On the other hand, it was not exclusively a Christian church. In fact, my only other personal experience at Shove Chapel was of Buddhist, not Christian, rituals. Years before Graham's service, I'd gone alone to see a group of Buddhist monks from Tibet demonstrate their religious practices, which primarily consisted of long periods of chanting as they sat upright at the head of the chapel. I had long been intrigued by Buddhism and had read quite a lot about it, so it was a rare opportunity to see actual practitioners in this land of Christianity. As the chanting resonated in the large, beautiful chapel, I was mesmerized.

Several years after Graham's service, I went back to the chapel one evening. The chapel was dimly lit and quiet. I thought I was alone until I walked down the hundred-foot central aisle to the front and began hearing soft chanting. There, off to the side in what is called the morning chapel, was a handful of people sitting in a circle and chanting.

Somehow, even with his sharp intellectual cynicism about organized religion, I think Graham would have appreciated the spiritual beauty of a few human beings seeking their own truth and acceptance of the suffering that is inevitable in this life. And this lovely human endeavor all taking place in this very special building, the same place where we all came one morning to say good-bye to a soul that was now, indeed, spiritual.

"There are more things in heaven and earth, Horatio, than are dreamt of in your philosophy."

– Shakespeare, *Hamlet*

Chapter 12:
HEAVEN AND EARTH

    Mary was raised in a fairly strict Catholic family, although her father was an Episcopalian. I was raised in an equally conventional Lutheran household, although my mother always said she should have been a Baptist and my father grew up as a Methodist. When Mary and I married in 1979, the wedding ceremony was conducted by a Catholic priest and Lutheran minister in an Episcopal church. As eclectic as all that sounds, there was no doubt our roots were deeply Christian and, thanks mostly to our mothers, we were raised in very religious households.

    Mary attended Catholic schools through sixth grade, then moved to the public junior high school. Given the lack of private Lutheran schools in the small Nebraska towns in which I grew up, I attended public schools but nonetheless had a rigorous religious upbringing. My mother led Bible readings and devotional sessions after each evening meal in our living room. From an early age, I was encouraged by my mother to become a missionary to carry forth the very important work of saving the souls of non-Christians worldwide. Without fail, our family attended church and Sunday school weekly - even on our vacations - a practice I did not break free of until I left for college.

In high school, I became a fervent almost evangelical Christian. I was the leader of our church's youth group and remember vividly going door-to-door late in high school to spread the good news of God. It wasn't until I started taking philosophy classes in college that I began to question the religious tenets I had assumed were correct when growing up. From then on, my questioning continued and my own personal views changed dramatically. It wasn't until much later I would learn that my own paternal grandfather, A.E. Stingley, was not a church-going gentleman and was not baptized until he was 81, just a few years before he died. Even later my mother told me about a philosophically rogue uncle she had who was an atheist.

I grew up thinking everyone either did or should go to church, and it took me some time to realize that this is not true; that my church can indeed be the woods and it is in fact okay not to conform to the prevailing thought of our culture. What was important was that in my own search for the truth I was honest with myself, that I asked questions and listened openly to the answers and that in the end I knew my own limitations for understanding.

My parents have remained deeply religious into their 80s, each in their own way, with my mother's outward devotion and my father's quiet conviction. "I'm not afraid of death," my father once told me. "But I am afraid of dying." And though the heated debates I once had with my mother about religion when I was young at some point ceased, I think my parents over time accepted that I had my own views of things, and they accepted that without trying to change me. After all, I think we all are looking for the same things: love and happiness while we're living and some clue, if not certainty, about what happens to us when we die.

Interestingly, Mary was on a similar path and early in our relationship we agreed about important philosophical and religious issues. She had a similar situation at home, a strongly religious mother and a quiet religious father. But as questions crept in for Mary, she veered away from the Catholic Church.

We loved to talk about and debate these things and did so for hours, sometimes late into the night sitting on a bench in the middle of the university campus. I remember these lively discussions with much fondness and much appreciation that I had someone like Mary to talk over our emerging views of the world.

This spirit of open and free thought carried on into our marriage and we agreed before we had children about how we wanted to raise those children. Mary and I fostered open discussion and debate among our children on such big issues as religion and philosophy. There was little dogma to guide the process. As a young couple, Mary and I had once shopped around for a liberal, open-minded church, first in Lincoln, Nebraska, and then in Colorado Springs, but in the end, only the Unitarian Universalist Church fit our way of thinking. Perhaps because of our church-going backgrounds, we seemed compelled to get our boys to a church, where they could be exposed to a systematic process of exploring and developing their personal spirituality, urged on by like-minded peers and teachers.

We attended All Souls Church fairly regularly while Graham was in elementary school. All Souls is a round-shaped, dark-brown temple situated less than a mile from Colorado College and Shove Chapel. The pastor was a younger, very amiable and intellectual southern gentleman whom I thought gave good sermons, always my favorite part of any church service. I enjoyed the church's eclectic, intellectual, and wide-open approach to religion, but even more, I enjoyed being there together with my family. It made me feel close to Mary and the boys in a way that was perhaps spiritually or intellectually different than what we ever had on a day-to-day basis.

After Sunday services, if the weather was nice, we'd often linger in the playground area behind the church. The boys would play while Mary and I soaked up the Sunday morning sun, watched, and talked. Then we would drive just a few blocks to Monument Valley Park, which spreads along

Monument Creek, past The Colorado College campus and the Old North End, with its big old houses and towering cottonwoods. At the park, the boys would again run and play on the swings, slides, and teeter-totters as Mary sat on the grass. Those were special days; sacred Sundays.

Despite the tolerant tone of those early church days—or perhaps because of it—Graham later developed a cynicism toward all organized religion that bordered occasionally on hostility. And yet for all his disdain of organized religion, he was fascinated by it. He and his closest friends were well versed in the Bible, its stories and characters, as well as the esoteric details of other religions. Graham and I enjoyed discussing and debating religion and philosophy, and would do so sometimes for hours, around the campfire on our backpack trips, driving in the car, or lounging in a hotel room when we traveled together. It was one of our favorite topics. Indeed, Graham may have loved the irony of his memorial service being held in a church.

I recently read that atheists were the most knowledgeable about religion, according to a Pew Research study. This was no surprise to me, and of course wouldn't have been to Graham, because becoming an atheist seemed to require a curiosity about religion, its underpinnings, and why people believe what they do. It's as my friend Donovan once told me, the more you know about religion the more clearly you can see truth. He is, by the way, the only person I know who has read fully both the Bible and the Koran, and he believes now in neither. "In my mind, we all end in the same place in the end, no matter what we believe in," he told me.

The Reverend Matthew Johnson-Doyle from the High Plains Unitarian Church conducted Graham's formal service, what little formal ceremony there was to conduct. I do think Matt said things that Graham would have approved of. Mary had cautioned him a few days earlier that we wanted a tone Graham would have been comfortable with. This meant avoiding the customary language and concepts of a Christian funeral. Mary had expressly forbidden Matt to use the word "heaven" in the service; there would be no talk of an eternal, blissful life. As a Unitarian minister, Matt had no problem with that. I remember vividly how he sat in the study of our home, attentively but quietly nodding his approval and acceptance of the grieving mother's requests.

What he did say remains a blur to me to this day, given my emotional state at the time. I do recall he debunked the whole notion of salvation that leads to an afterlife, saying something about not being able to offer up a "fairytale" about where Graham's spirit might be headed. I remember cringing a bit at those words, not because they didn't express our or Graham's feelings, but because I knew that most people in attendance, especially my own family, would vehemently disagree. In the end, though, I was comfortable with what was being said because this was for Graham, after all. Others in the building would have their own funerals one day, with different kinds of spiritual concepts and different kinds of spiritual leaders. Everyone would get his or her own day at the chapel.

About a year later, I attended the funeral services of a friend's mother. I was struck by how much I could relate to the Lutheran funeral service, with its familiar language and quiet sense of reverence. As I sat in the blond wooden pews of this church, I felt transported back to my childhood and recaptured the same warm, calming feeling I'd had as a young boy, sitting in similar blond pews.

The differences between the Lutheran service and my son's were striking. And though the sense of sadness and loss was the same, in many ways they could not have been more opposite. The first thing I noticed was that the focus was not so much on the deceased's life, but on the religious beliefs of the church. The pastor spoke at length of the various saints involved and how and why these saints would convey the dead person's soul to heaven, where the person would live happily for an eternity under the care of God. It was as comforting a scenario for me as it had been when I was a boy growing up in Nebraska. Likewise, hearing the story again must have brought immense calm to the grievers in their confusion and sadness. I sat and listened and could feel the pleasant energy of the church as the pastor spoke slowly, clearly, and confidently to these people who believed in these beautiful concepts of eternal salvation, eternal happiness, and the rejoining of loved ones after death. The language used to address death fascinated me, and as I looked around the small church I could see that my fellow souls were reassured. I envied their comfort. I wanted their peace.

But as much as I admired the scene and respected what was unfolding, I felt awkward because I did not believe these things. I wanted to believe, in a way that ran deep in my own soul, because it seemed so right and so perfect. It demystified death. It made death not only understandable, but acceptable, even attractive. But I had lost that kind of faith many years ago, and so far have been unable, even unwilling, to regain it.

"Sometimes it's bad when the going gets tough, when we look in the mirror and want to give up, sometimes we don't even think we'll try, sometimes we cry."
– Van Morrison, *Sometimes We Cry*

Chapter 13:
A LETTER FROM POPS

On February 23, 2005, Graham's service unfolded slowly and solemnly in the beautiful stone chapel, into which he would never tread, on the campus of a college he would never attend. Nonetheless, his life and spirit seemed to fill the chapel to the apex of the fifty-foot-high, arched ceiling.

In the front of the chapel, at a dark grand piano, sat Colonel Jim Burling, the father of two sons who were very close to all my sons, particularly Will and Graham. He flawlessly played "Clair de Lune," a breathtakingly beautiful song. I've listened to and appreciated music played in all kinds of styles by all kinds of artists in my life, but nothing was ever as beautiful as Jim playing that song on that piano.

The gathering silently listened as the piano notes reverberated around the chapel. Months after this poignant moment, I researched the origin of "Clair de Lune." Not knowing French, I had no idea at the time what the title of the song meant, but of course the meaning of those words should have been obvious to me looking back. It means "light of the moon." Even later, I would search for and find a poem written in the mid-1800's by the same name. I'm not sure if the poem is what the composer of the song, Debussy, based his original classic work on, but the poem was as poignant for me as the music at Graham's funeral. Like so much art or music I have been exposed to since Graham's death, it seemed to speak directly to my hurting self. The poem was written by Paul Verlaine.

Claire de Lune

Your soul is a chosen landscape
Where charming masked and costumed figures go
Playing the lute and dancing and almost
Sad beneath their fantastic disguises.
All sing in a minor key
Of all-conquering love and careless fortune
They do not seem to believe in their happiness
And their song mingles with the moonlight.
The still moonlight, sad and beautiful,
Which gives the birds to dream in the trees
And makes the fountain sprays sob in ecstasy,
The tall, slender fountain sprays among the marble statues.

During Graham's service, Mary's sister and three brothers all gave eulogies, as did Graham's friend, Karl. They provided everything from humorous glimpses of Graham's quirky behavior to his love for his family, friends, and this beautiful world we all still lived in.

His good friend, Karl, spoke, using his lifelong nickname for his best friend.

I don't think Grahama would want me to ramble on, so I'll make this brief.

I learned a great many things from my friend Graham. I learned to play the guitar and to appreciate the music of Bob Dylan. I learned that pushing a station wagon down Mount Herman at seven in the morning is not as easy as it sounds. I learned that the road trip is as much about the drive as it is about the destination. But above all, I learned that no matter what a man does in his lifetime, it is the things he leaves with the ones he loves that really matter. The thing that Graham has left with me is a sense of pride in the fact that I have been given the last eight years to make his acquaintance, and this experience has profoundly changed me.

I became friends with Graham in a time of great struggle and leave him in the same, but his spirit is what always helped me get through these times of grief and I'll always be indebted to him for that. So in every pint of Newcastle and every pack of Lights, I'll think of my friend Graham and the times that we spent living the life that wouldn't have been possible without him.

Several others walked to the front to speak of Graham. One uncle, Dan, spoke of Graham's unconventional and independent personality. "I'll never forget the time the entire Winter family was flying somewhere on a trip, and Graham walked into the plane in his slippers. My kids loved it," he said. "I loved it."

Another uncle, Wint, gave a thorough and touching tribute to his nephew, ending of course with my wish not to put Graham on a shelf, so that his spirit could last forever in the hearts of those who loved him.

I had written a letter to Graham in the days since his death, and I had asked another of Graham's uncles, Adam, to read it, because I knew I could not. He walked up the grand stairs at the front of the chapel, then slowly to the podium, pulled the folded papers from his suit jacket, and deliberately and flawlessly read aloud the letter:

To my oldest son, Graham:

Your birth opened a door for me that no one else could have opened and was the reason your mother and I had three more sons. You gave me hours of joy as you grew and played and asked questions about the world, many of which I could not answer. You were curious and sensitive from the beginning.

I watched in wonderment as you were nurtured by your mother, and as you gave her such a beautiful love in return. I saw this relationship between you and your mother flourish from the first few moments of your life. From the time she nursed you as a baby to the last days of your life.

And I experienced an ever-deepening and respectful relationship between the two of us, as I matured as a father and a person. The things we loved and shared grew.

Your relationships with your brothers would take volumes to describe, because they were so rich and complete. I admired you and your brothers' unique relationships, seeing you grow closer and closer to sweet Will, seeing you finding joy and laughter with special Seth, and seeing you form an unquestionable bond with Colin. Of course, there were your sad-eyed friends, Molly, Scooter, and Sally [our pets].

I saw you develop friendships with your peers and your elders alike that won't be forgotten by those who got to know you. Even though you felt sad, you made others feel happy.

And we all hurt that you are now gone from our everyday world.

I saw in you a deeply complex human being, who experienced some joy and a lot of pain. I smiled often for you, and I hurt for you often as well. It was never easy for you.

You were my philosopher, my cynic, my reader, my intellectual, my rebel, my nature lover, my master of language, my musician, my firstborn, my beautiful, beautiful son.

Your body seemed to fail you from the beginning. The surgery when you were a baby to give your skull a chance to grow. The emotional depression that we recognized when you were in third grade and started to treat. The depression that I think you had to fight your whole life. The athleticism of your youth that seemed wasted later. The constant and severe headaches and stomach problems. The constant, bittersweet effects of your many and ever-changing medications.

I heard you say many times to me in many ways what Bob Dylan sang so plainly: "I can't stop this pain in here."

I thank the many doctors who tried to help you feel better; I thank the teachers and everyday people of your life who saw who you really were and reached out.

The night after your soul passed from your body, I looked at the night sky you loved and saw a beautiful yellow moon. It made me sad, because you could no longer see it with your own eyes. But it made me happy, because it seemed as though the moon cast the light of your spirit and it shined on me. I think I will see your spirit in the moon every night until my own death.

The pain and suffering and awareness of your hurting soul and the frequent harshness of the world also made you such a special person to me, your mother, your brothers, and others who knew you. The part of your personality that was such a burden to you—your sensitivity—could also bring out the best in you. From your sorrow came kindness, gentleness, sincerity, realness, honesty, and an awareness of others' pain.

It makes me sad and confused to think that there is some part of your life that I will never know fully. I ache to know just how you felt. I ache at the mystery of your death and what you must have gone through. What were you thinking, and, more importantly, what were you feeling? What horrible confusion and pain were you experiencing? How alone you must have felt. Did you know you were going to die? Did you want to die, or did you want to live?

You were like other brilliant and tormented men who could no longer cope. Some of the same writers, poets, artists, and musicians you admired: Ernest Hemingway, Vincent Van Gogh, Edgar Allan Poe, Kurt Cobain, and Hunter S. Thompson.

And like those men, you are gone now, but you have left me and the world so much.

A LETTER FROM POPS

Graham, I will always love you.

—Pops

"My son, a perfect boy...had ended his earthly life. You can never sympathize with me; you can never know how much of me such a young boy can take away. A few weeks ago I accounted myself a very rich man, and now the poorest of all."

– Ralph Waldo Emerson

Chapter 14:

SYMPATHY CARDS

In the days following Graham's death, one thing that impressed and overwhelmed me were the cards we received in the mail. They came by the dozens, many with heartfelt, meaningful, and helpful things to say. Frequently, people would mention their experiences with Graham and how they enjoyed knowing him. Others who didn't know Graham would say very nice things about our family. A few sent longer letters expressing their feelings about Graham, our family, or both.

One letter that especially sticks with me came a few weeks later from Gary Brown, a high school teacher who had taken a liking to Graham. I believe Gary had been a computer teacher for one of Graham's early classes. They also both loved basketball—Gary was the high school varsity coach before we arrived in town—and music.

Coach Brown wrote:

Mary and Steve,

Forgive me for not getting in touch with you sooner, but I knew that you would need time for yourselves and time for the many family and friends that wanted to try to give a touch of comfort in their own way. I figured that an old coach and friend could wait.

I can't imagine the feelings that you have with losing Graham, so I will only say that I am sorry. If there is anything I can do, please let us know. I have to refuse to concentrate on the loss because it hurts too much, and I hope you understand that I want to honor Graham through the years to come with thoughts and stories of the happiness he brought to me and certainly to you.

As a teacher, I have seen many students over the years, and knew and have forgotten many names and faces over the years. Some students leave you with a small memory, some, none, and yes, a few you can't wait to forget.

Then there is Graham. From the moment that I first met him, I felt like we had a connection. I don't know if I can perfectly describe that connection, because of course I don't know Graham's thoughts, but I will try and give my side in hopes of giving you a few moments of joy knowing the effect your loving son had on me.

There is no forgetting Graham! There wasn't a moment of time that I didn't enjoy being around him and talking to him, even the times when I felt like I was doing most of the talking. I remember the change that I saw in Graham at school when his physical appearance started to mirror the trouble and the battles that he was obviously waging inside, and many people at school noticed the dreary dress…I'm not very good with words, so forgive the use of an analogy here, but what I saw can best be described not clouded in darkness and despair, but in terms of many rays of light shining in many directions; just, for whatever reasons, not able to focus in one brilliant outwardly visible, beautiful light that I feel Graham was capable of producing and would have if he hadn't been taken from us so early.

I guess I feel like I always had one of those rays of light shining on me from Graham because we never had cross words and I always got a smile. Our conversations about sports, life, and himself were always humorous and thought provoking, even at his early age. I think I liked Graham so much because he reminded me of a part of myself; way more going on inside myself than I can successfully express or convey to others in the way that I should. I honor your son because, with all he had to battle, he was still to me much more successful in uplifting me than I feel I was to him, and I honor both of you for the type of boy (man) that I saw in your son, as a direct result of the love you had for him.

Some of what we as individuals can hope for is that when we are gone, we have affected people for the better and that we have provided for the ones we love, so that we will be remembered with gladness and love. Know that your son has done that for me, and I am sure that he has for you. The letter that you wrote, Steve, is one of the best tributes that I have heard and confirms that Graham will live in your hearts always with happiness and love.

You have a wonderful family and I have enjoyed watching and knowing your boys.

Sincerely, "Coach" Brown

Others expressed similar feelings, if not as eloquently as Coach Brown. It was as if our community produced a blizzard of sympathy cards, something I will not forget. A few years later, after our children had left the nest, Mary and I briefly discussed whether we wanted to make Monument our home for the rest of our lives, a place we'd lived in since 1985. The easy answer was yes, and that was in part because of the love expressed by this community toward us.

The cards, however, could not relieve the pain and the confusion of having lost our son, which were simply overwhelming. And there were occasions when the words or actions of a well-intended friend or neighbor would show they had no real understanding of what we were going through.

SYMPATHY CARDS

Ironically, it was when people seemed self-assured about the meaning of this horrible situation that they sometimes came across as insensitive or even rude.

A few general themes kept coming up in the cards. Many tried to reassure us that our memories of Graham could and would bring us peace and even pleasure in the future, if not now. Others tried to soothe us by reminding us we would see Graham in heaven when we died.

Neither of these pieces of advice was helpful, at least in that time of extreme emotional distress. The existential dread of the moment was all we could feel. The notion of seeing Graham in heaven was implausible at best and arrogant at worst. Images—let alone memories—of Graham opened and reopened raw wounds.

A simple flash of a memory of Graham doing anything, anytime, with anyone, was excruciatingly painful because it reminded me that he was no longer alive. It reminded me that there would be no new memories. There would be no memories of Graham getting married, having children, having a career, coming to our house for Thanksgiving, or simply watching a movie or sitting down and talking about his day. Seeing the pictures that were put together on the poster boards for the memorial was unbearable for all of us. There he was at six, smiling and standing on a hill above Breckenridge with the summery Rocky Mountains in the background. There he was, reading a book with his headphones out in the yard of a rented house in Jamaica, where we had vacationed just a few years ago. There he was in his purple soccer uniform, proudly looking at the camera, smiling big, with a ball tucked under one arm.

To look at any of those photos made me wince with pain. Mary didn't look. She couldn't stand to see his face, so alive and happy. Of course, a day would come when it would be easier to see pictures of Graham, and eventually, we did begin to slowly and delicately bring pictures of Graham out into the open, placing them on the fireplace mantel or hanging them in the hallway of our home. For the first few months, I remember only one visible picture of Graham in our house. This photograph sat on the side of a desk in our kitchen, and showed a happy Graham wearing his black Wayfarer sunglasses, sitting on a sailboat off the coast of Italy during our vacation just the summer before.

At the time, such images and memories didn't salve the wound in my heart; they merely reopened it. Maybe one day the memories of Graham would make me happy, make me feel fortunate that I shared twenty-three years with him. But that day was not now. Now, all I felt was sadness. I was staring into the irrevocable fact that Graham was gone. There was no getting around that simple, horrific truth. I was not happy that all I now had were memories, only memories.

"You have disappeared, you have been released, you are flecks of light; you are the mist. Somewhere spinning 'round the sun, circling the moon, traveling through time, you are mist."

– Lucinda Williams, *Copenhagen*

Chapter 15:

FROM THE GUY IN THE SUIT

With his friendly smile and his direct manner, Graham always had a way of getting along well with adults. One special relationship he had during his middle school years was with Ted Belteau, the middle school principal who was an equally friendly and direct southern gentleman about my age. It wasn't until several years after Graham's death that Ted and I had a conversation about his relationship with Graham and how special it was. I asked Ted if he would write something about it and later that same night he emailed me his recollection

Graham

I can't tell you exactly when Graham Stingley walked into my life, but I can remember the exact moment when I heard he walked out. It literally took my breath away and made me feel ill. I had to leave the meeting I was in and go to the restroom to re-compose. But that is not what I want to share. I want to share a verbal picture of the Graham I knew.

I first heard of Graham from my daughter, Bree, who was the sitter for the Stingley Boys. She would come home raving about how fun they all were...Graham, Will, Seth and Colin. I heard the names so often I felt like I knew them before I ever met any of them. As the Middle School principal in Monument all of them would pass through that educational setting and Graham was the first.

Like I said...I can't remember when Graham first ended up in my office. I don't remember it being for discipline, it seems more like he asked to see me for some other reason. There he was...tall, blond and smiling. The minute he entered I saw him look at the Pez dispensers lined up on my desk and he said "cool." One word, but it conveyed so much and was an indicator of where our relationship would be going. "Have a seat and help yourself," was my response. He was the first kiddo that ever sat in that chair by my desk and emptied an entire dispenser of its candy goodies. Most would take a tab or two...but not Graham...he emptied it and was eyeing another until I said, "that's enough sugar before you go back to class or you're going to be bouncing off the walls." He laughed and we talked about whatever the reason was for him being there. I told him if he ever needed me just ask to come and see me and then he strolled out and went back to class and I went back to work. I would see him in the hallways and lunchroom as I made my rounds and always got a smile and a wave.

Not long after that first meeting Graham asked to come see me and his teacher sent him down. He came in and this time no smile, no "cool" just "Mr. Belteau I need your help." I have no idea why he trusted me or knew that I would be there for him, but I do believe that dogs can predict storms and that kids intuitively know who they can trust in times of turmoil and I was blessed to have Graham trust me. Again the reason for needing my help is not as important as the fact that he came to me. Actually he told me that sometimes he just felt really anxious about school and didn't know how to handle it. This was a 7th grader describing his feelings to a guy who usually had to deal with gum chewing or pushing in the hallways not anxiety or fear. I asked him if he wanted his counselor and I will remember forever what he said. "No, you told me if I needed something to come to you and here I am." I don't know if I should thank God or Fate or some other "entity" for sending him to my office. In reality, I guess I should thank Graham for taking me up on my offer. After that talk that I won't share here (I never shared it with Mary or Steve either, because it did not involve any worry on my part about his safety or any other topic they needed to be apprised of...in fact it was pretty mundane middle school stuff...but to Graham is was important which meant it was important to me) I went to each of his teachers and told them if Graham ever asked to see me they should allow him to do so. I also said if he ever used me as an excuse to get out of class or to avoid a class assignment I would end his "right" to come to my office when he felt the need. I told Graham the same thing. He never once abused his visit time with me. Over the next school year and a half I spent time with Graham almost every week or so. Sometimes he came to talk about music, sometimes to talk about basketball, sometimes to ask about why certain things were certain ways in schools/politics/life or some other topic that was on his mind. Once he came to ask me why I wore a suit every day. That question still makes me smile and laugh because it was so Graham. We had great talks even though most only lasted 15 minutes or so. I truly doubt that I did anything for Graham but here is a partial listing of things he did for me...

1. *He made me think before I answered*
2. *He made me laugh when laughter was the best response*
3. *He made me realize why I loved middle school kids*
4. *He provided a reality check for me on a regular basis*
5. *He told me about new bands and music*
6. *He got me to remember my days as a semi lost and confused middle school kid*
7. *He made me feel needed*
8. *He shared himself with me*
9. *He spoke of his folks and brothers with love and he had a passion for the world more than a passion for things (and he would love that I stopped at #9 instead of going the easy way and having 10 things on this list).*

When Graham left the middle school and went on to high school I saw much less of him, but it seems like every time I was at the high school I'd bump into him and every time he would see me he would come over and shake my hand (this was before the days of "man hugs") and we would talk for a bit and it always ended with me saying "tell your family hi and if you ever need me just call, I'm in the book." He never called, but over his high school years we had a few "meetings" each year and every one of them left me smiling and feeling better about myself and about the youth of the world. Graham Stingley was a bright, colorful light in my world and he still is. When someone special leaves your presence they leave behind part of their energy and I feel Graham's energy on a regular basis. I have no idea what happens when we check out of this hotel we call "life." But I do know this...whenever those I have loved have "checked out" I still feel them close and I still feel the love they sent my way. I feel Graham's love for me and I believe he feels mine for him. I was the lucky one because of the time I had with Graham and I truly hope he felt the same about the time he spent with me. Peace and love to you Graham from the guy in the suit.

"Oh man, take care! What does the deep midnight declare? 'I was asleep—from a deep dream I woke and swear—deeper than day had been aware. Deep is its woe—joy—deeper yet than agony: woe implores: Go! But all joy wants eternity—wants deep, wants deep eternity.'"
— Friedrich Nietzsche, *Thus Spoke Zarathustra*

Chapter 16:

VISIT TO THE MORTUARY

A couple of days after Graham's death, it became my task to visit the mortuary where his body had been sent by the Denver coroner's office. I quietly took this task upon myself after a very pleasant woman from the mortuary called our house and said someone had to come down and "make the arrangements." Mary was in no shape to come with me, and I certainly didn't want Graham's brothers to be a party to this horrid errand.

This was no time for a family outing.

I called the woman and made an appointment to meet with the people at the mortuary to discuss my son's cremation and what to do with his ashes. Driving down to the mortuary in Colorado Springs was itself a strange experience, because I hadn't been out of our house in a few days. The mortuary was a windowless, cinderblock building just off a busy, north Colorado Springs thoroughfare. The building was a stand-alone structure in an old strip center with some marginal businesses, such as a laundry and bicycle repair shop. Nothing but a treeless expanse of parking lot surrounded the strip.

As I entered the mortuary, the very first thing I saw was a small, sterile chapel, where the churchless people of the community apparently had their funerals. Inside the chapel, several people were preparing for what appeared to be an impending funeral. At the front of the chapel was a casket.

A professionally dressed woman, who seemed practiced in being friendly and cheerful but serious all at the same time, greeted me. She took me into a room, where I sat alone until the manager of the mortuary came in, dressed in a suit and tie. He said it had been a "bad week" for young people dying. He said my son had not been alone in his suicide, because several other young people had killed themselves that week. He went on to recount a few details of the suicide of a woman younger than Graham.

I was shocked. I told him very promptly and firmly that my son probably had not committed suicide but had died accidentally, probably due to an unintended, lethal mixture of prescription and over-the-counter medications. We talked briefly about the circumstances of my son's death, but the mortuary manager seemed undeterred from his previous assessment, as if someone else more knowledgeable had informed him differently and I was the mistaken, shaken father.

He then leaned toward me as if he had something important to say, shook his head slowly, and said softly to me, "In my experience, I see people who try to figure out why things happened, and my advice is not to do that. Don't try to figure it out. It will drive you crazy."

We moved into an adjoining room, this one with a variety of urns, all labeled with names and model numbers for easy reference. I picked one of the simpler urns. I then completed some paperwork and purchased the services required under these circumstances. In my state of mind, the experience was not unlike buying Graham a used Saab just a few months back. This time, though, there was no car, no Graham.

I arranged to have a lock of Graham's long, golden hair preserved, as

Mary had requested.

As I left the mortuary, I thought about the mortician's advice. Good advice, I suspected, but I couldn't accept it. Why had he thought Graham's death was suicide? The question nagged at me. After all, the coroner's office had concluded that it was not a suicide, although they listed the official cause of death on his death certificate as "undetermined."

As I drove back home, my mind reeled with the possibilities. I was beside myself, not knowing what had happened to my son. I had to have information, as dreadful as any information would be. I had to know the truth.

The next day, I sat near a phone in my home and summoned the courage to call the coroner's office for the City and County of Denver, where an ambulance had delivered Graham's body on February 18, 2005. They told me it would be a few days before they had the autopsy results. After several phone calls back and forth to the coroner's office, I finally connected to the doctor handling Graham's case, Dr. James W. Wahe. It took more calls before he was ready to provide me with some results. This was an agonizingly slow and macabre process.

Finally, a week or so after Graham's death, I sat in my office at the bank in Monument listening on the phone to some guy I didn't know talk matter-of-factly about my son's death and what might have been the cause. First he told me he'd ruled out a heart attack or any kind of heart problem. They hadn't found any illegal drugs or alcohol in his system. There didn't seem to be anything in his body that provided a clue to his demise, he reported to me. It was a mystery, and he would have to do some additional blood tests before he could determine the official cause of death.

After several phone calls to this office of death, and this final conversation with Dr. Death himself, I couldn't take it. I was emotionally wrung out. I called my brother-in-law and asked if he would continue these conversations with the coroner, because for one of the few times in my life, I just could not carry on with the task at hand.

I also kept thinking about why the police had searched Graham's apartment on the morning of his death. Most likely they were looking for illegal drugs that might have caused an overdose. They apparently scoured the apartment for clues and found none.

Then, a day after Graham's memorial service, a clue surfaced.

On that day, Mary's three brothers and her father rented a U-Haul truck, drove to Graham's apartment building, and proceeded to box and load up all of Graham's possessions. In the process, Mary's brother, Adam, went through Graham's kitchen trash and found a small bottle of cold and flu medicine, a generic brand bought from the 7-Eleven across the street from Graham's apartment building. This was reported to me by Adam, who said he recalled finding an empty bottle of the medicine in Graham's trash. There was a receipt attached to a paper bag that showed Graham had bought the medicine just a few minutes after he left us that night at the downtown brewery.

This news seemed to explain a lot. Graham was so sick that he'd stopped on the way home to buy a generic version of Nyquil. Most grocery and convenience stores have their own brands of this medicine, which all have the same ingredients: acetaminophen for relieving pain and fever; dextromethorphan for suppressing coughs; pseudoephedrine for decongesting the nasal passages; and doxylamine succinate, an antihistamine to allow better breathing.

The problem with these drugs is that they are well known to interact very negatively with the particular antidepressant Graham was prescribed, which, as I've explained previously, was a monoamine oxidase inhibitor (MAOI). The MAOI Graham was taking was called "Parnate," the same drug his mother had been using for some time.

Any one of these cold medicine ingredients can have bad side effects, but the real culprit is the pseudoephedrine, a decongestant. Pseudoephedrine is one of the key ingredients in homemade methamphetamine, one of the most dangerous, addicting, and deadly illegal drugs around. In his recent book, *Beautiful Boy: a Father's Journey through His Son's Addiction*, David Sheff gave a complete description of just how awful and tormenting this drug can be. Pseudoephedrine is so onerous that Congress passed a law restricting its access, which was signed into law by President Bush in 2006. Then, in 2009, Colorado and several other states further restricted access to this drug, allowing its purchase behind the counter only, and requiring some personal information from the individual buying any medicine that contains pseudoephedrine.

Interestingly, on a trip to Amsterdam years after Graham's death, my youngest son Colin and I stopped at a pharmacy there to get Colin some medicine for a bad cold he had at the time. As we asked the pharmacist for possible medicines he could only offer pain killers. "I'm sorry but anything with pseudoephedrine is illegal here in the Netherlands," he told us. "It has been that way for some time."

As we walked out the door after buying some simple ibuprofen, Colin was upset because he couldn't get anything stronger for his cold and I was upset knowing Graham might ironically have been safer in Amsterdam, where he once thought of going to school, than he was back in America.

"Where has that old friend gone? Lost in a February song. Tell him it won't be long, 'til he opens his eyes, opens his eyes."

– Josh Groban, *February Song*

Chapter 17:

CAUSE OF DEATH

In 2010, I went to a local grocery store's medicine section and found out I could only buy a generic "nite-time multi-symptom cold and flu relief" medication, as well as name brands of similar medication containing pseudoephedrine, by taking a purchase ticket to the pharmacy to purchase. About the same time, I also made a visit to the 7-Eleven at Nineteenth Street and Arapahoe, where Graham had bought his medication the night of February 17, 2005. With my heart pounding and my head dizzy, I walked into the store where Graham would have last been before he died that night. I looked in vain for a medication that contained pseudoephedrine, even one that could only be purchased behind the counter. Instead, I found several name-brand cold and flu medicines for sale, all with absolutely no pseudoephedrine.

In an curious twist, the drug that probably killed Graham had been pulled out of all 7-Elevens by a bill passed by Congress and President George W. Bush on March 6, 2006, not much more than a year after Graham's death.

When I learned of the empty bottle of cold medicine found in Graham's trash, I concluded that Graham had drunk the entire bottle of the cold medicine, either willingly, carelessly, or accidentally, and this medicine had interacted with his antidepressant and killed him.

Mary's brother Adam relayed the information about the bottle of cold medicine to Dr. Wahe, who subsequently did some more tests to determine the levels of both the over-the-counter and prescription medicines in Graham's body.

His findings were inconclusive.

On Graham's certificate of death, in the section labeled "manner of death," the only box checked was "undetermined manner." Elsewhere on the certificate, the coroner wrote, "Mildly elevated levels of therapeutic and over-the-counter medications of uncertain significance." In yet another spot, the doctor wrote, "Possible combined therapeutic drug toxicity or adverse reaction." Eventually, Graham's death certificate would be sent to me with the word "undetermined" typed in the space allowed for the official cause of death.

What the coroner *did* find were appropriate traces of Parnate, Graham's MAOI antidepressant; Depakote, Graham's headache-preventive medicine; and Klonopin, Graham's anti-anxiety medicine. All these drugs were found in Graham's body at prescribed levels. In addition, he found "slightly elevated" amounts of pseudoephedrine and "elevated" amounts of acetaminophen, one of the other active ingredients in cold medicine. Neither of the amounts found in his body were high enough to kill Graham, the doctor said.

"What about the cold medicine in combination with the antidepressant, anti-headache, and anti-anxiety medicine?" Adam asked him.

Possibly, the doctor responded, but there was no way to tell for sure.

On March 4, 2005, Adam e-mailed me:

Steve,

I just spoke to Dr. Wahe for ten minutes. Before calling, I found the correct spelling of "Axert" and verified online that it was a migraine drug. I added it to the list of drugs he was taking, as there were open tabs around the room (maybe three). It also appeared that he had taken Topamax fairly recently, so I added that to the list too. I also added over-the-counter Imodium and generic Nyquil, as it was clear to me he had taken those drugs recently.

I asked Dr. Wahe if he had been there when they picked up Graham, and told him that I was no expert, as I was a banker, but in my common-sense opinion it looked to me to be an accident, and not intentional suicide, as I entered the apartment. His response to that was "Yeah, well, the panel we ran is supposed to pick up everything, but Graham was on so many meds that it didn't get all of them. His alcohol was negative (no alcohol in the bloodstream) and there were no illegal drugs. Like you, my hunch is that this was a drug interaction and not intentional overdose. In our experience, when there's a suicide, there are very elevated levels of drugs (i.e., people swallowing a whole bottle of pills). It doesn't appear at this point that this is the case with Graham."

"Let us first be as simple and well as Nature ourselves, dispel the clouds which hang over our brows."

– Henry David Thoreau, *Walden*

Chapter 18:

INTO THE DESERT

In April 2006, a little more than a year after Graham died, I packed my camping gear, coaxed our young golden retriever, Sophie, into the back of my SUV, and headed south into New Mexico. My mission was to get outside alone to try to make some sense of the past year. This trip also was an opportunity for me to revisit the Gila Wilderness in the far southwestern corner of New Mexico, where I had gone some thirty years earlier as a young college student. As I did then, I sought again now to flee my everyday life; to un-clutter my head in the rugged mixture of mountains and canyons, an absolutely beautiful and desolate place. For all its grandeur, it was one place where I knew I would see few, if any, other hikers. I wanted to be alone with my thoughts.

On my trip to southern New Mexico, I stopped first for the night at a house our family owns in Taos. It is a peaceful place, set with other adobe-style homes on a broad mesa overlooking the Rio Grande Valley to the west and the Sangre de Cristo Mountains to the east. I love the region because I'd explored it first when I lived in Santa Fe in the late 1970's and then with Mary after we got married in September 1979. New Mexico, with its piñon-covered hills and far-away, sweeping mountains, is an aesthetic and spiritual place for me. It draws me back frequently. I have found peace and refuge there.

But this trip was different. There was no peace and refuge. My mind was deluged by thoughts of death and questions about my son's death. That first night of my trip, I sat by the fireplace in the Taos house and read from a book given to me by my friend Jerry Mahoney. *The Denial of Death* was written by Ernest Becker in 1974 just before he died of cancer at the age of fifty. It's a fascinating and very detailed look at modern-day man's existential situation, his attempts to find meaning in life, to deny his inevitable demise, and finally to come to terms with his death.

After reading for a while, I wrote in my journal:

Death

Death, now there's a concept and something to think about, eh?
Mr. Death is here
He always has been
And it seems to me
Always will be
He doesn't like to be seen
Even if you look real hard
He vanishes just when you
Think you can glimpse him
But he's here
And Everywhere
All around the world
Everyday
Tonight, tomorrow
And yesterday I saw him
I touched him.

The next day, I sorted my camping gear on the clay-tiled floor as I sipped my coffee. Then Sophie and I continued our journey south to Albuquerque, where I would go to a Bob Dylan concert with a friend. Those were the few moments I spent with another person on that trip. This was a friend from my childhood, someone I stayed in touch with, albeit infrequently. He had lived with his wife and kids on some land in the low mountains east of Santa Fe ever since he'd graduated from art school and became a carpenter.

In Albuquerque, I found a funky-looking old motel that would take Sophie for five extra dollars over the regular $19 rate. When Mary and I traveled, we stayed in nice places, so this was an interesting change for me. I enjoyed the simplicity of my worn and dirty room, plus the added attraction of seeing people I wouldn't normally bump into. There was the drunk Navy veteran who stood in the parking lot in the evening, sipping from his plastic cup as he rocked gently back and forth. Next to me, it looked like an entire Mexican family lived in one of the tiny motel rooms. I could see their makeshift kitchen through the front window. Then there was the "crazy woman" who lived on the second floor of the motel. I got these facts from a woman who knocked on my door soon after I checked in. She was friendly and said she wanted to see my beautiful dog. She chatted about all the people who lived in the motel and offered to walk Sophie in a nearby park while I went to the concert, information she pulled out of me as we stood in the doorway of the motel room. I politely refused her offer, but she pursued the possibility of "all of us" walking in the park the next day. When I found another friendly offer written on a note placed on my windshield the next morning, it hit me that she was a prostitute, albeit a coy one.

In that early morning, I set out on the empty highways of southern New Mexico toward a rugged, remote mountain range in the southwest corner of the state.

At the concert the previous evening, I had looked to my side almost expecting to see Graham, and instead it was my friend. Some strange mistake had swept my son away so finally that he could not again stand by my side. During those past concerts with Graham, I had felt a special connection to him, as we enjoyed the same music in the same perfect moment. Now, I felt disconnected from those around me, even somewhat disconnected from myself, as if I had been ripped out of the world I used to inhabit, the world that held all my sons.

As I drove south, the beauty of the piñon- and then cactus-covered hills was astounding. This was a land I had come to love when I moved here so many years ago as a young man, younger than Graham had been when he died. Yet now the beauty of the place seemed distant to me, focused as I was on my swirling thoughts. I stopped at one point to write in my journal:

Do I think so much of Graham that I am less connected to my other sons? Sometimes I don't feel connected to anyone, even to myself. Am I floating through life, not really feeling it and experiencing it? I know better than to live this way. It's what the Buddhist teachings I have read warn against, but I may be missing the point. And now it seems so silly to even try to "live in the now" and be happy with my son dead. What point is there in trying to be happy? Because I don't feel like I really can. It seems that I will always be sad and terrified that one of my other sons will also die.

Sophie and I reached our trailhead into the Gila Wilderness in the mid-afternoon sun. From there we hiked through the desert hills. As I set out, I quickly remembered how raw and tough this country was. The trail was steep and rocky, with little shade from the bright desert sun. Sophie, still not much more than a puppy, soon lagged behind me, her tongue hanging out and her panting quickening. When I stopped to give her a break, she headed quickly to what little shade there was near the trail.

My own body heated quickly, and sweat poured down my face. My mind was a swirl of thoughts, let loose by the solitude, the quiet, and the walking. I thought about what others might think if they were walking up the same trail at the same time. Mary had recently told me she sometimes floats in her own mind, her body seemingly unanchored to reality. I wondered if that was how Graham had felt at times. How unnerving that would be.

I thought about what I was doing and why I might be doing it. I remembered listening to Bruce Springsteen with the boys when they were young and, much later, listening to the "Ghost of Tom Joad" with Graham west of Buena Vista after camping. The words "sitting around the campfire with the ghost of Tom Joad" brought to mind how I'd be sitting around the campfire with the ghost of Graham Stingley, and what that might make me feel or think, and how I wanted to understand Graham's death. I probably couldn't, I knew, but I wanted to clear everything away and try to see more clearly. I wanted to at least try.

As my thoughts wandered, I suddenly remembered dreaming of Graham the previous night. I had dreamt that he was okay, and that I was so relieved that he really hadn't died. What a wonderful feeling it had been. And then I'd woken, and the awfulness of his being gone all rushed immediately back into my head.

Then, just as suddenly, I was remembering looking for pictures of Colin in the basement for his high school graduation party just a few days earlier. In my search I couldn't help but see pictures of Graham. I noticed how happy he looked as a young child, and how unhappy and stressed he looked as he got older. I actually noticed it, to a lesser degree, in my other sons. When did it get worse for Graham?

Eventually we reached the top of a cactus- and pine-covered ridge that offered spectacular views both to the east and to the west. There, I set up my simple tent and built a fire. I cooked my evening meal with my small stove. And as if nature was determined to provide me with special entertainment for the night, the sun set in the western sky just as an enormous moon rose on the eastern horizon, orange and radiant. I took in the show, sitting on the quiet ridge, sipping from a flask of whiskey, with Sophie curled up by the fire asleep after the long hike.

I pulled out my journal and wrote,

Was I too hard on Graham when he was growing up—especially when he was very young? Was I too easy on him later because I felt guilty? He was undisciplined, and maybe that is because I was undisciplined with him. Could he not see my example? I'm getting defensive because I don't want to feel responsible for his unhappiness and his sadness during life. On these trips with him in the past he would sleep a lot during the days, sometimes until mid-afternoon. Why was that? Did he feel so bad about life that he would rather sleep through it? Was he so drugged that he couldn't stay awake even if he wanted to?

I miss him so.

"Somethin' filled up my heart with nothin', someone told me not to cry."
— Arcade Fire, *Wake Up*

Chapter 19:

I WISH

On the morning of April 13, 2006, I awoke just in time to see the full moon set on the western horizon, as it had the morning after Graham's body was found in his apartment. I stood on the ridge, surveying the view on all sides. As far as I could see in every direction there was nothing but small, pine-covered mountains, split occasionally by deep canyons. The sky was clear of any clouds. I could see not one sign of man. Despite being surrounded by the rugged beauty, my mood was very different than it had been the day before. The exuberance I had experienced then was gone. It seemed like a common pattern for me emotionally in those days: feeling relatively happy and content, only to succumb to feelings of sadness and despair. Maybe it was as simple a formula as feeling bad when my thoughts were stuck on Graham's death and feeling better when those thoughts receded. Particularly when I was alone, my thoughts would get stuck on those topics that made me feel the worst. And here, in the middle of the Gila Wilderness, I was truly alone.

It's not that I wasn't comfortable being alone. In fact, I normally enjoyed solitude very much. My everyday life was typically filled with people: family, friends, and coworkers at the office. So being alone occasionally was a pleasant change. But being alone also brought with it an opportunity for introspection that could be all-consuming. It was a time I could use to sort through the inner files of my mind, undistracted by conversation.

That April morning, like many others, I couldn't shake the notion that I was somehow responsible for Graham's death. At one point on the trail, I reflected that he'd camped with me just to do something I enjoyed. In other words, he followed me, trusted me. And I let him down by not being someone he could trust. It made me feel horrible to realize this. As kids, all my sons had trusted me, and I'm not sure I was ever worthy of that trust. And in Graham's case, I felt the trust was fatal.

I broke my small camp and, with Sophie just ahead of me on the trail, hiked away from the ridge and over several mountains before reaching a steep canyon edge where the trail led us down to the only flowing stream within miles. The stream, Mogollon Creek, was about twelve feet wide but only a few inches deep. It provided an oasis in this very dry country. I had been running low on water, with only about ten ounces to get me the five miles to the creek. Sophie was so excited to see the creek that she headed directly into it, lay down, and drank off and on for half an hour. She loved the water. I filled my now-empty water bottles. I sat down on a rock next to the creek and gulped down the cold and refreshing water.

It was still except for the soft sound of the stream and the songs of a few birds. Sophie and I sat in silence. I pulled out my tiny stove and brewed some coffee, my first of the camping trip. The sky became overcast with very high, thin clouds, so I was sure that night would lack the stars-and-moon show that had entertained me the night before.

Then, for some reason, I thought about the few heart-shaped rocks I had seen on the trail during my hike. They reminded me of Will. As a young child, he would get so excited whenever he found heart-shaped rocks on our hiking and camping trips. In his boyish voice he would point out the rock to me and his brothers, smiling proudly as if he had just discovered a gold nugget. We took many of those rocks home with us. I still look for them whenever I hike. Maybe it's because they remind me of the magic of that first time Will found one. Maybe it's because a heart rock instantly reminds me of Will's personality, his gentle, kind soul, quiet but expressive when it counts most. As with my other sons, it will be interesting to see how Will's life will unfold as he gets older. And like Graham, they are each in their own unique ways as brilliant as beautiful as any father could hope for. Most of all, I hope they are essentially happy and outlive me.

I don't want to lose another son.

Sitting there on the rock, sipping my coffee and watching the creek flow by, I realized that despite all the bad feelings I had about losing Graham, I did still sometimes feel good about my life and some of my accomplishments. Having children and being a good father—not withstanding Graham—was at the top of the list. Also, my marriage—and remarriage—to Mary and our relationship had generally been good and rewarding, hopefully serving as a decent role model for our children. And I felt that I'd been a supportive companion to Mary, helping her with her life issues, especially since she'd had such a difficult time with her own identity, her relationship with her parents, and her ability to cope with the world around her. It had been a two-way street too, because I knew Mary loved me like no one else in the world, and always has and always will. I'd never doubted this, and I looked forward to living out our lives together with that basic foundation of love. Mary's not perfect, but she is the most deeply loving person I know.

And then there was me as a person. I felt I had lived an interesting life. I had worked at keeping engaged with the world, whether through my career; through arts like music, art, photography; through the natural world; or through my own intellectual world of reading, writing, and just plain thinking. Physically, I'd kept myself in relatively good shape and appearance. I had a good sense of humor and an aura of optimism—although these two things were harder for me to really feel after Graham died.

I also reflected that I was truthful in things that mattered. But sometimes I found myself joking and being "happy" when in the company of others, and then I'd catch myself and realize I was doing that out of a life-long habit rather than true feeling. I knew I had a hard time expressing the sadness that I live with every day to others, even to Mary and the boys. I found I presented myself as okay emotionally when I really wasn't. On the other hand, I knew that as I grew older and more mature, and certainly since Graham's death, I was finding it easier and more natural to show the real me. I still had difficulties talking about Graham, but at least I wasn't *always* all smiles when I didn't feel it.

Out there in the wilderness, I reflected that maybe that's why it was so easy for me to be by myself—because I didn't have to put on a "Steve show" for anyone or, conversely, try to express what I was *really* thinking or feeling. I thought about how this struggle at least partially stemmed from my upbringing. My parents, to this day, are models of optimism and express this as their role, as when my dad recently spoke of his commitment to "stay positive," a veiled reference to Graham's death. He urged me to do the same "for your other boys," if nothing else. I reflected on that, while this optimistic stance wasn't necessarily bad, it created a climate in my early life in which I was discouraged from readily and freely expressing myself, especially if what I had to express was negative. But of course, much of what anyone feels about life is negative. There are a lot of horrifying, troublesome, and worrisome aspects to life. To say otherwise is to lie; to deny the power of death.

On the other hand, I thought, dwelling on death couldn't bring much good to your psyche and certainly couldn't do anything to bring the dead back to life.

What is done is done, I thought. I couldn't bring Graham back to life. All I could do was honor his spirit during the rest of my own life.

The next day, hiking down the high-desert trail from Mogollon Creek back to the trailhead, I composed a poem in my mind and wrote it down when I got to the car.

I Wish

I wish you were me
That you could be here now
Gliding down the trail
Enjoying the view and the feeling of being outside
I wish I could hear you say,
"Yes, Pops, I'll go camping with you"
I wish I could have understood
More of what you were going through
And why you were suffering
I wish I could have shown
My love more to you
I wish I could have made it better
I wish you were still here
For my sake,
For the sake of your mother
And for the sake of your brothers
I wish you could have married and had children
What a wonderful father
And husband and lover
You would have been
I wish you hadn't had depression
Or headaches
I wish you had been
Happy and carefree and worry-free
I wish you could have had
The good fortune of health
Like I have and you didn't
I wish you hadn't had
To take so many medications
God knows the help and hurt
They caused your body
I wish you could have been an athlete

*Or a musician
And felt some sense of accomplishment
Not for my sake, or the world's
But for your sake alone
I wish you could be alive
And I could be dead
That is what I wish.*

"What good am I if I say foolish things and laugh in the face of what sorrow brings, and I just turn my back while you silently die - what good am I?"
— Bob Dylan, *What Good am I?*

Chapter 20:
WHAT GOOD AM I?

Driving home, I tried to clarify in my mind what I had experienced on my trip. I wanted something real and helpful to take home with me. But my experiences had brought forth nothing new. I had experienced the same internal thoughts and feelings that I brought to the trip: sadness over Graham's absence; confusion and disbelief accompanying that sadness; guilt that I hadn't done more to save him; a sense of failure at one of the few endeavors I really care about and want to be proud of—fatherhood. I wanted to be a good father, one who protected and nurtured his sons and didn't let them feel unhappy or get hurt or die. That thought continued to haunt me. Somewhere, somehow, I'd messed up bad.

I'd thought the trip might lessen some of my pain. I was aware that my grieving couldn't be resolved, then or ever, but I was hoping I could get just a notch or two more understanding and clarity about what has happened and my role in it. Really, I wished I knew about Graham's life in general: what it was and wasn't, and what his actual experience was and why. I'm not sure I got that extra notch that trip, but at least having the time to write, think, and feel was helpful.

The only revelation I could recall was as simple as it was profound: no matter what I did or felt, Graham was gone and I couldn't bring him back. I also thought a lot about my other sons and their futures on this trip. I was excited about what time would bring to their lives. It wasn't their fault that Graham was gone, so to the degree that I could, I wanted to fully engage as their father.

And I thought a lot about Mary, of all the good things we had to look forward to despite this burden we had to bear upon our souls with every breath we took. We did have our other children, and though they were leaving or had left the nest, I was sure we'd be an intimate part of their lives and would share their experiences as they grew, matured, and entered the real world as educated and civilized young men. We had the material structure of our lives—like our house and our ability to travel and have nice things—that would help smooth life's rough, nasty edges and give us some comfort and enjoyment. More importantly, we had each other to help get us through this risky life full of peril, hopefully with some fun and smiles along the way.

As I drove, my thoughts drifted randomly with little interruption from the outside world, although my parents did call me on my cell phone. My mother said she hoped I'd go to church the next day.

I spent some time thinking about how intelligence causes as many problems as it resolves. Intelligent people, like Graham, seem destined to be tormented by a world that often makes no sense. Later, I would read in a story in the *Wall Street Journal* about a study done by a Tufts University School of Medicine professor of psychiatry that showed people who suffered from depression were more realistic and empathetic. The study by Dr. Nassir Ghaemi concluded that people who suffered depression had a much sharper sense of reality. They were therefore better leaders, because they could see what really is and not what psychologists call "positive illusion," which gave non-depressed people a higher self regard and slightly inflated sense of how much control they had of the world around them. Dr. Ghaemi cited examples such as well-known depressives Abraham Lincoln and Winston Churchill in a book about the study, called "A First-Rate Madness: Uncovering the Links Between Leadership and Mental Illness."

Sense or nonsense aside, I returned from my trip into the desert wilderness with perhaps more understanding of my grieving but with few tangible resolutions to my feelings. I would continue to get outside and alone as much as possible in the months to come, in short respites to clear my mind and make at least some sense of what I had been through. But very little clarity came my way.

"Remember when you were young? You shone like the sun. Shine on, you crazy diamond."

– Pink Floyd, *Shine on You Crazy Diamond*

Chapter 21:

ANGEL WITH A PONYTAIL

In our family room once sat a light-brown couch, covered with soft leather that had faded in the harsh Colorado sunlight. It now sits in a storage room, waiting to be used by one of my sons as they settle into homes or apartments of their own. This couch has many memories for me, but none as powerful as that of Graham sleeping on the couch during his lunch breaks when he worked as a teller at our bank.

During that time, we'd often take lunch together at home. Normally I'd arrive a few minutes before him, and I'd eagerly watch for Graham's silver Saab buzzing up the driveway. In a few moments, he would invariably come in the front door and head straight for that couch, heave his tall frame onto—and seemingly into—it, and take a forty-five minute nap. His morning's work seemed far more stressful for him than for other tellers, and, exhausted, he would begin his nap without stopping to eat lunch. He'd lie on the couch in his sweat-soaked, starched dress shirt. Actually, the shirt was one of mine, and it was too large for Graham.

We wouldn't exchange words during this lunchtime ritual. There was no time for that. I'd sit at the dining room table and eat my lunch and read the newspaper. And from time to time, I'd watch my son sleeping soundly on the couch, in his ill-fitting shirt, the smashed end of a tie—also mine—peeking out from under his body as he lay on his stomach.

This motionless, exhausted boy had, only hours before, dazzled all those whom he came into contact with, whether they were customers or fellow workers, old or young. Graham could "put on my business personality," as he called it, in a way I've yet to see matched, and I have worked over the years with many people.

For example, I remember once hearing Graham greet an elderly customer with a firm, clear, and respectful tone. "Good morning, sir, how are you doing today?" I imagined the customer looking up to see this cordial greeter, and smiling back at him, pleased with the unexpected exchange.

It was interesting to watch these interactions from another perspective; to consider the irony of a ponytailed young man charming the socks off our conservatively dressed bank customers. But with Graham's personality, the differences melted away, and a human connection was made between two souls, probably both with their share of earthly burdens.

Not infrequently, someone would show up at my office door with a compliment for my son. They would praise his customer service, his friendliness, and his charm. They would call Graham a "nice young man" and so forth. I thanked them for their praise and was filled with pride.

After Graham died, one of my now-retired colleagues shared his impressions of Graham. In high school, Graham held a menial, mindless filing job at our mortgage company. He had a small desk in the back of the office. "He was very sweet to me," this now-retired colleague told me. "He was a very nice person, and people enjoyed having him around the office."

It was simple: people loved Graham. The problem was, I think, that Graham couldn't really *feel* that. He was stressed and pressured by his everyday exchanges with humanity. He seemed disappointed by his abilities to deal with people, but also, quite frankly, by people in general. So Graham hid his social discomfort with an exceptionally pleasant manner.

This was the cause of his collapses on the couch at noon. This was the cause of the sweat staining his shirt. "See, this job is so stressful it drenches my shirt with sweat, Dad," he would say as he lifted his arms.

The happiness Graham brought to others he could not bring to himself.

There were days Graham could not go to work at all. He would wake with a bad headache and stay in his dark room upstairs all day, sleeping. It stressed me, because I was running a business in which I expected the employees to be reliable, and yet my own son was often late or absent. People were kind about this, but I knew it created an unseen problem within the company.

The opinions of others aside, my own heart would ache with sympathy whenever Graham called in the early morning to say he couldn't come in to work. I knew he only felt worse about himself because of these episodes, and I felt so sad and helpless.

Nothing was better than those days when Graham came to work with me at the bank, making me and the others feel good as well. Even when he was pushing the limits, wearing slippers to an early-morning, all-staff meeting or reading the *New York Times* on the Internet at his workstation, he brought a vibrancy and energy to the entire bank.

And from time to time, he would take a break from the teller line, stride into my office, sit at my guest chair, and say, "What's up, Pops? What are you working on?" It was a moment that made my day every time. I would simply look up at him and say, "Not much," stare into his smiling, brilliant eyes, and feel that nothing could be better about that moment. Nothing.

Cindy Wehlage, the manager of the bank branch where Graham was a teller, wrote me a letter several months after Graham was gone:

When I first started working at the bank, one of my first customers was a boy with long, blond hair and big, bright eyes. He dressed all in black.

He was polite and kind, but very quiet when he spoke. I waited on this boy probably three or four times before someone told me he was one of the "owner's" sons. This I would have never guessed. He didn't expect to be treated any other way than any other customer. Time went by, and a couple of years later Graham came to work for us. He had worked at several other locations and in other departments of Peoples. Having Graham was nice because he was already trained and eager to go. Graham had a natural way with the customers. Customers latched onto him very quickly, and I envied how he could remember their names so easily, not to mention remembering special things about the customers. No wonder they liked him so much! It wasn't long before Graham and I became working buddies. Graham would greet me with that great big smile and a "Cindy Way!" He had a great sense of humor. He never failed to do what we asked of him. It didn't matter if it was helping customers, answering the phones, carrying heavy boxes up from the basement, or finishing off a sandwich. And Graham was the man to go to when I couldn't reach something on a high shelf. A high five was always in order as we passed through the lobby or hallway. Sometimes he would hold his hand up so high I would have to jump to reach it, and then he would let out a big, goofy laugh. I really have missed those high fives!

Several people thought that Graham should cut his hair, that it really wasn't appropriate for a banker to have a ponytail. I was proud of Graham for standing his ground. I always giggled when, after the doors of the bank closed, the first thing he would do was to let the tail out and shake his head. One of my most favorite ways to pick on Graham was to walk by his desk or chair and tug at his ponytail...I would hear a "Hey, now!" I told him that it was the only way I could keep him in line. One time he asked me if I was mad at him, and I asked why...he replied, "Because you haven't pulled my ponytail lately."

Sometimes when I was frustrated or having a rough day, there would come Graham with a Coke. He would say he went to get something and had extra change that he needed to get rid of. Some mornings I would get onto the interstate after dropping my son off at school, and there would come Graham, zooming around me. Of course, I couldn't let him beat me to work! That would have just been wrong. He would wave, and the race would be on.

There are so many great things and stories about Graham that it is hard to know what to put down. Sometimes Graham would come into my office for no reason but to chat. This was fun, because he almost always made me laugh. Sometimes he would be a little down or tired, so he would just sit for a minute or two. He would tell me what wonderful things his brothers had done in basketball or whatever, and say, "I wish I were like them." What a proud big brother! If Steve was out of the office, Graham would ask, "Where's Pops?" or "Anyone seen the Pops?" This made me laugh too, because I always pictured a "Pops" to be a very short, rather round man...

I hope as my own boys grow older they speak of me as Graham always spoke of Mary to us, in a kind, loving, "my mom is the greatest mom in the whole wide world" way. There is not a doubt in my mind that Graham's family meant love to him. At Graham's services, I listened to the loving words that he had written about his mother and the rest of his family. What wonderful expressions these were! When the moon is full and bright and the stars are shining, I see a little bit of Graham because of the words of his family. I become attached very easily to the people I work with and who are kind to me. People come and go, in and out of our lives. Graham, however, is a person who will always have a special place in my heart. I, as many others, am a better person for having known him. I know we will meet again someday and I can't wait for the high five from the angel with the ponytail!

"Oh my brother, your wisdom is all that I need, oh my brother, don't worry about me. Won't you tell me my brother, cause there are stars up above."
– The Head and the Heart, *Lost in My Mind*

Chapter 22:

THE AMBASSADE HOTEL

In the summer of 2004, our family took a trip to Europe. Mary and I had been there before, but it was our first visit with the whole family. We flew to Germany, then took the train south over the Swiss Alps to our destination, Finale Liguria, a picturesque region on the Italian Riviera. We spent close to a week there, at a hotel propped on a steep hill overlooking the Mediterranean, which spread out gorgeously below.

The photographs and memories from that trip—our last big adventure ever with all six of us together—will endure a lifetime.

From the Riviera, we flew to Rome and spent a few days, before Mary and the three younger boys flew back to the United States. Graham and I took a side trip, first to London for a few days and then up to Amsterdam, where Graham, a friend of his, and I had been a few years before. It was one of our favorite cities, probably for quite different reasons. Graham loved the Bohemian feel and the brown coffee shops that openly sold marijuana. I loved the culture and the ambiance of a city whose buildings—none over five stories tall—line quaint canals. Not to mention the free-flowing Heineken at every sidewalk cafe.

Graham and I checked into the Ambassade Hotel, a fifty-room hotel in the heart of the city, and climbed the stairs to our shared room. It was going to be a wonderful week. I wrote in my journal on August 5, 2004, "Okay, top floor of the Ambassade Hotel, room 33, with a view of the leafy trees and the canal and the old Amsterdam building across the canal. Now I'm set. Now I'm alive. Now I'm happy."

We spent our days walking and riding bikes around the city and in Vondelpark, the large, shady park at one end of town, eating at sidewalk cafes, and going to art and other museums (including an eye-opening and heart-wrenching visit to the Anne Frank Museum, which Graham wanted to see, just up the street from our hotel.)

After eating dinner out, we'd end up in the room each night, drinking Heineken and talking. We listened to music on a tiny set of speakers propped up in the open windows of the room. I spent some time fretting about Graham, his depression, and his solemn disposition, but mostly I just tried to calm my worried mind and enjoy his company, without a parent's sense of judgment and concern.

"I'm trying to relax here and now and enjoy this very special time and place," I wrote in my journal. "It will soon be gone."

I did miss Mary and the other boys. "I feel bad that not everyone is here, or that I'm not doing this one-on-one with my other sons. I want to strengthen my relationship with all my boys. I'll have time to do that in the future," I reminded myself.

On August 6, 2004, the day before Graham's twenty-third birthday, which would be his last, I wrote, "What a significant day tomorrow is. Some twenty-three years ago in Omaha, Nebraska, he came into my world. And to think of all the changes that have come to his life and to mine since then. Last night, Graham said to me that he should 'grow up' someday, but for now he is okay with still being a 'child.' That pretty much summarizes where he is and what causes concern for both me and his mother. I wonder when he will grow up."

Of course, the days at the Ambassade came to an end, and we made the long flight home. I wrote in my journal how excited I was about the future. The boys were progressing and changing, and the future looked so promising for them all, even Graham, I hoped. As I stared out the plane window at the expanse of ocean, clouds, and sky, I wrote, "The view from here is very nice, let me tell you." I sketched that window view in my journal, which I still look at occasionally. When I do, I can feel the optimism, the happiness, of that special time with Graham.

On the next page of my journal, I wrote down a lyric of the Bob Dylan song I was listening to at the time on my iPod. It was more ominous: "Time is an ocean but it ends at the shore," he sang. "You may not see me tomorrow."

I would return in 2011 to the Ambassade Hotel, this time with my youngest son, Colin. He was curious about my trip with Graham, and asked me questions about the details of that time. I tried my best to shake myself of those memories and create a new set of memories with Colin, but at times it was difficult and we both could feel the pull of sadness that Graham was gone and those good times with him, as a son and a brother, were not to be repeated.

Oh, just to be able to sit in a quiet Amsterdam coffee shop and have a conversation among the three of us, Colin, Graham, and myself. Or rent bikes and ride through the Vondelpark together. Oh what I wouldn't give for that opportunity.

"And I could write it down and spread it all around, get lost and then get found and you'll come back to me, not swallowed by the sea, you belong to me not swallowed by the sea."

– Coldplay, *Swallowed by the Sea*

Chapter 23:
A SURPRISE E-MAIL

More than five years after Graham's death, I learned a startling new piece of information about the cause of his death. Dan Winter, Graham's uncle and Mary's brother, offered to review the manuscript of this book. I eagerly took him up on the proposal, because Dan was well-read and knew the English language as well as anyone. In addition, and probably more importantly, Graham and Dan had been close, particularly later in Graham's life. Besides being extremely literate, both were fiercely independent, intelligent, and opinionated. They also both—at least at that time in their lives—shared a penchant for smoking marijuana, sometimes together.

No more than twenty-four hours after I e-mailed my rough manuscript to Dan, he fired back an e-mail to me. He had stayed up nearly all night and read the entire manuscript. He had many things to say, but the very first line made my heart pound as I read it, for it clarified something I had been confused about for years. It was a subtle but very significant change in the facts as I perceived them.

Dan said he needed to correct my understanding of the discovery of the cold medications in Graham's apartment. I'd understood that they'd found the empty bottle in the trash of Graham's apartment, next to a 7-Eleven bag with a receipt attached. Dan wrote in his e-mail:

"The part about the receipt is correct. It was time-stamped just after he left you at the restaurant. But about the following, I have a crystal-clear recollection and have relayed it to others several times: the generic, 7-Eleven Nyquil bottle was not empty, and it was not in the trash. It was on the table next to the sofa in the living room. I found it there and showed it to Adam and Wint, and we discussed it.

"The bottle had the lid on it, and the little plastic cup into which you measure a dosage was sitting right next to the bottle. There was a line of dried medicine on the sides of the cup, indicating that one dosage had been carefully poured into it. It was very clear that one bottle had been bought and one dose had been taken. The bottle wasn't empty. It was nearly full. It wasn't in the trash. It was on the table next to the sofa.

"That was the point, when I examined the bottle, that I felt certain that Graham didn't mean to die. When I processed the meaning of that carefully measured generic Nyquil, I was sure that Graham hadn't committed suicide."

Sitting in my study reading the e-mail on my laptop, I was stunned. Mary was sitting next to me, but I didn't have the courage to tell her right then and there what her brother was telling me, because I thought it would be such a powerful time and situation to suddenly recall. I stayed silent, but I kept rereading Dan's e-mail. It was months later that I actually brought the email up to Mary and to my surprise, she wasn't surprised. She took the news calmly, quietly, and then after thinking about what Dan had written, went into a different direction.

"Maybe Graham was so depressed he *did* kill himself," she said to me. "Maybe he was just that depressed."

It was a strange twist, because I had been the one that had thought that originally, only to slowly but certainly change my view. In the days after Graham's death, I somehow had the impression that the bottle of cold medicine had been empty and in the trash, and therefore Graham, either through an act of carelessness, recklessness, or willfulness, had ignored all caution and prudence and ingested the whole bottle the night before he was found dead. He would have done this knowing that several ingredients in cold medicine could interact with his antidepressant and cause all kinds of problems, including death. He knew better, I'd told myself over and over in the years since his death. He knew better and yet still swigged a bottle of poison.

Now, everything was changed. Graham was not reckless or careless. It was quite the opposite. He had been literally and figuratively measured about taking this medicine. If he had wanted to hurt himself, he wouldn't have taken the time to slowly and carefully fill the measuring cap just to the right line: the line of appropriateness.

The poor kid was sick and wanted some relief before going to bed. That's all.

Dan went on,

"I looked at the apartment with fresh eyes from then on as we cleared it out. In fact, I looked at it very keenly because I was, until that point, too heartbroken to allow myself to really see anything of Graham's there. It was all too surreal and we were all three committed to just getting the job done in that '*Winter way*,' cleanly, quickly and completely, because we couldn't bear to personalize the contents of Graham's apartment.

"While Adam, Wint, and Karl dealt with the bigger pieces, I concentrated on the drawers, closets, and kitchen and dresser drawers, looking to make sure nothing of special, personal, sentimental value would be lost. I knew Graham was an accomplished weed smoker, but there was no weed in the apartment. There were packets of rolling papers and a quantity of seeds and lots of lighters. There were no beer bottles in the trash (several in the fridge) and the apartment appeared neat and clean, not inconsistent with that of a young dude who had a sense of pride in his pad. His closet was neat. Trash had been recently emptied. Graham had been purposeful in the days before he died. Taking medicine. Taking out the trash. Picking up the apartment. Folded clothes. Shoes lined up in the closet. Books lined up on the shelf. Hadn't even been getting high. (A cold or the flu never stopped me from getting high—it actually helped the symptoms.)

"I kept thinking I was going to run into drugs or some paraphernalia. For someone who had experience with different drugs, I would not have pegged the owner of that apartment as a big drug user. The only references to drugs—and I looked carefully everywhere—were the seeds and the papers. I was really surprised that I didn't find his stash of weed or something else. But nobody had been drinking or getting high for at least a couple of days in that place. Back then, I was getting high daily and I know what a daily smoker's place looks like. I don't know what a soon-to-be-suicide's place looks like, but that place looked like the resident planned to be around a while."

Now, I'd known Graham smoked pot. I had been around him a few times as he smoked. I had been around it when we had visited Amsterdam and had pushed him several times to quit. I thought maybe it was making his depression worse. He disagreed.

"It's my antidepressant, Dad," he retorted after one of my attempts to warn him of the dangers. "It's the only thing that really works for me, the only thing that makes me feel better."

I found out later from Graham's friend Karl that Graham had called him the night before his death to ask if he had any pot, and Karl said he did not. Who knows, maybe it would have made him feel better. Maybe it would have saved his life.

Not long after Graham's death, Colorado moved to legalize medicinal marijuana. Literally hundreds of shops selling marijuana sprang up virtually overnight, several within a short walking distance of Graham's apartment building. I know people who ingest marijuana to relieve their depression and reduce their anxiety. Maybe, just maybe, if those pot stores had been open for Graham that fateful night, he could have purchased cannabis instead of the deadly cold medicine that was loaded with the active ingredients of methamphetamine. And maybe he would still be alive.

Dan's e-mail continued:

"My point is this: the apartment looked comfortably lived-in. It was neat and clean, the medicine bottle was carefully used. Nothing looked careless once I started really looking at it. It didn't look like the person who lived there was going to check out. It didn't look haphazard. The appearance of the apartment was consistent with a guy who smoked a bit of weed, loved his family (he saved all his cards and letters from them), who was battling the flu and had just stepped out.

"In short, the 7-Eleven cold medicine on the table, the lack of a plethora of drugs, no evidence of recent drug use, the neat, clean appearance of the apartment—I'm not an expert, but it didn't seem like the place of a guy who didn't intend to continue to use it. I've thought of suicide numerous times in the past and each time, I was fucked up. Drunk or stoned or zonked on pills. There wasn't any way he could have been any of those things—as the toxicology report showed. And the careful measurement of that cold medicine—that was what cinched it for me. He was trying to make himself better, not kill himself."

I tried not to let my eyes tear up as I read Dan's email. I didn't want Mary to be concerned. She'd been through so much and I felt in some ways she was beginning to heal after all these years. And she blamed herself for Graham's death, because he had been taking the same strong and very interactive antidepressant that she had. "He was too young to be on that medicine," she told me once, tears streaming down her face. "He shouldn't have been on that medicine. I shouldn't have let him be on that medicine. It's all my fault."

Crying into my chest, Mary felt a pain no parent should feel. She felt a pain she did not deserve to feel. "My baby, my poor baby. He was too young."

"So wise, so young, they say never live long."
— Shakespeare, *King Richard III*

Chapter 24:
A DEATH IN NEBRASKA

Months after Graham died, long before Dan's revealing e-mail, my mother called me one day to tell me of a couple in her church in Lincoln, Nebraska, whose oldest son had died in a very similar way to Graham. Their names were Joyce and Dick Clark, and their oldest of two sons, Kerry, had died at about the same age as Graham. Like Graham, Kerry was living alone in an apartment, going to school, and struggling with depression. Also like Graham, Kerry had been on an antidepressant and seemed to be dealing with the depression, but had fallen ill with flulike symptoms, and after being sick for a few days, had taken cold medicine.

After an extended exchange of e-mails and a meeting in person, Joyce and I came to the conclusion that the deaths of our sons were remarkably similar. They even both occurred in February, although seventeen years apart.

It was helpful, though painful, for me to hear Joyce's story. She wrote to me,

"I'll spare you the details, but Kerry was prescribed an antidepressant by a psychiatric doctor at the Medical Center. He struggled through classes and work for a few more weeks and finally in late November he decided to quit school and not finish the semester. We encouraged him to move home until he could get back on track, but he was still determined to do it on his own and stayed to work in Omaha. We were in touch with him often. He almost didn't come home for Christmas, but he did, and we're so thankful, because it was the last we had with him. He started feeling better and enrolled for second semester in January.

"He rebounded well, and about a week before he died, he called us and was enthusiastic about what he was doing again. He said he'd finally found his real niche: he wanted to go into pediatric intensive care when he graduated. He loved little kids and related well to them. It didn't surprise us at all! He'd had lunch with his woman instructor, and she confirmed all this to us, too, at his funeral."

Then there were the gut-wrenching details of his death.

"Monday came and he didn't make the expected suppertime call…We tried calling him. There was no answer, but it was not unusual for him to work someone else's shift at the ER, so we figured that was where he was. I stayed up most of the night and kept calling and getting more concerned. When he didn't answer by 7:00 a.m. Tuesday, when I knew he should have been getting ready to go to an 8:00 a.m. class, I called his newly married friend. He was concerned too and agreed to go check on Kerry. He's the one who found him dead in bed, called to tell us, and called 911.

"We were also told later by ER coworkers that Kerry had called in sick for work Saturday night, and on Sunday when friends talked to him, he said he was dizzy and didn't feel good. Never in his life had Kerry ever complained about being dizzy, sick, or otherwise, or used that word. Scott found him dead in his bed, in pajamas, and said it had been a struggle and was not a peaceful death. He assured us that Kerry had left no notes."

Joyce had made the same assumptions that had entered my mind after

Graham's death:

"Well, you know the devastation that took place after that phone call. Since Kerry was taking the antidepressant and this had happened so suddenly, without warning, suicide was our first thought. Even though he was better, without really thinking, we assumed something had tipped him over the edge. No matter how it had happened, we couldn't believe he was gone. It's still hard to believe at times…

"Since the circumstances of his death were questionable, [an autopsy] was required, and they didn't need our okay, since he was twenty-three. We discovered the police had confiscated all medications from his bathroom and around his apartment. They somehow missed taking a bottle of Robitussin DM, the over-the-counter medication he was taking. His apartment looked lived-in as usual, nothing out of the ordinary, and interestingly, he had bags of groceries to last him a couple weeks still on the kitchen table. He'd put the perishables in the refrigerator. We were not prepared to deal with any of that, locked things up, and went back to Lincoln to prepare for a funeral."

Trying to figure out what had happened ate at these parents:

"People would stop by or call while we were there and assured us that Kerry had been doing well and they saw no signs of suicide; he was talking positively about his family, that he had come out of his slump, all things to uplift us. Of course, in the back of my mind I wondered if they were just saying that and knew something else. I got it in my head that I needed to see what the police had taken, and I have no idea now how I accomplished that. I called someone beforehand, and Dick and I went to the police department. After being treated like a couple of criminals, we were taken to a basement evidence room and brought a small paper bag. There were no surprises, other than they had also taken the cat's medicine too. The bottle of antidepressant was there and according to the label and contents left, we were able to determine Kerry was pretty much on schedule taking them. We were relieved, but still puzzled.

"Some months after Kerry's death, we were sent the complete, very descriptive autopsy report; painful reading for us, and there was no one to explain to us what it really said. The cause of death was listed as accidental overdose, but we didn't know why they had come to that conclusion, because they didn't know what he was taking."

Finally, after more than a year of trying to find out things on her own, Joyce made an appointment with a psychiatrist who was knowledgeable in pharmacology.

"When we met, we told him what had happened and asked him to look at the autopsy and see if he could interpret it for us. He looked at it for no more than a minute, and the first words out of his mouth were, 'Well, for one thing, this was not a suicide.'

"We were stunned! He went on to explain that if had Kerry taken an overdose of his antidepressant, it would have shut down his digestive tract and they would have found a clump of pills. There were no pills or any evidence of Desipramine (his antidepressant) found in his digestive tract. The blood work indicated a high presence of the antidepressant. [The ingredients in] over-the-counter medications were also present, but neither of us remember just what that [medicine] was. We recalled finding the bottle of Robitussin DM, and [the psychiatrist] said [the ingredients] would have been in that or any cold medication he might have taken. That was the only one we were aware of, and the police had none in their possession either. He said that the active ingredient in the cold medicine, whatever it was, made the body retain the antidepressant until the levels turned toxic and killed him. It would have made his heartbeat irregular and according to the psychiatrist, 'His death was an adult form of sudden infant death.'"

The Clarks then met with the dean and a doctor at the medical center where Kerry was a student. They confirmed, after looking at the autopsy, that his death was not a suicide as they had thought.

"When we got up to leave, the dean looked at us, and I'll never forget what he said: 'If I've learned nothing else today, it's that we should never assume again that when one of our patients dies that it was suicide.'

"We had a great weight lifted from us that day and it truly was the beginning of my healing. I remember crying all the way from Omaha to North Platte."

"Death, the only immortal, who treats us alike, whose peace and refuge are for all. The soiled and the pure, the rich and the poor, the loved and the unloved."
— Mark Twain, *Note left at his deathbed*

Chapter 25:
AN OMINOUS EVENING

There are only a few times in my life in which I have been so emotionally shaken that I could not stand. I felt physically crumpled, unable to go forward, unable to do anything. Time and the world around me stopped, as if it were my last moment to live. Having had the luxury in my life of not having to have ever confronted death directly because all my family was alive and I had not even lost a friend, it seemed now for the first time I was staring death directly into its hollow eyes.

This moment came the late fall of 2004, just months before Graham died. He and I were spending the evening home together at our house. Mary and my youngest son were out for the evening. Will and Seth were away at college.

Graham and I had decided to spend the wintery evening in the hot tub on our back deck, a favorite hangout for me and my sons. The sun had just gone down, and the brightest stars were beginning to appear. Graham sat on the west side of the hot tub and I on the other side. His long hair was tied up above his head so as not to get it wet. Warm and relaxed in the water, I searched the sky for constellations from the high perch of our wooden deck. Though there was a slight glow from the lights of Colorado Springs some fifteen miles to the south and from Denver some fifty miles to the north, for the most part the night sky above our house was dark and clear. As usual, Graham and I talked about the beauty of the evening, and perhaps even identified the first planet or two we could see. Graham knew far more about what was out there than I did, and he often would explain which of those first shining lights were coming from planets.

But, unusually, Graham soon began to talk very seriously about his life and everything that was wrong with it. At first, I tried to engage in the conversation, but soon I stopped. The thoughts and feelings Graham expressed were so intense and so awful I couldn't speak. I could not respond. I could only listen in horror. Graham was so eloquent and so open about how he felt. He listed all the ways in which he thought he had failed, was currently failing, and was going to fail in life. I don't remember all the details, because there were so many, but I remember some, like earning poor grades, not having a girlfriend, and not playing sports. He also talked about how he could not see life getting better and that the only thing that gave him hope was the idea that at some point soon he would no longer be alive.

When he was finished after about twenty minutes, I could not talk. I was stunned. My son's complete, absolute expression of failure and hopelessness was simply overwhelming for me as a listener. As a father, it filled me with despair. I sat in the hot tub, not knowing what to say or how to express what I was thinking or feeling. I remember vaguely that when Graham was talking, there was this awful silence. And then I think he got out, leaving me in the hot tub alone. I sat there for a while, tried to collect myself, and could not. I can't remember a time when I felt so overwhelmed and unable to cope.

When Graham had expressed similar feelings in the past, I'd always attempted to be positive about his life, his problems, and his hopelessness.

I would say things that I really believed: that his life would improve; that he was truly, deeply intelligent and capable; and that these abilities would get him through life and even help him thrive someday. "Just hang on and it will get better," I would tell him.

But not this night. I sat there in the hot tub, alone, crushed. I was a man who could not deal with what had just been said. They were not just words, but the true, horrible expression of what my very own son was feeling in the core of his being. There was zero hope in him in that place and time. And it was staggering.

To be confronted with that kind of utter depression right then and there is one thing, but to know that Graham felt these things almost constantly is another. I will never know what was in his mind; it's impossible. But I can imagine that he felt this kind of hopelessness often—and that the feelings were just as overwhelming and all-encompassing as what I felt that night in the hot tub. Even when Graham seemed happy or engaged in the world, I believe these feelings were inside him, pulling him down. It was not only the severity of his thoughts and feelings, but also their constancy that was so awful.

Afterward, Graham and I spent some time apart in the house, though I can't remember what we did. I do remember that somewhat later I heard Graham's muffled sobs from his temporary bedroom upstairs.

I went into his room, sat on his bed, and leaned over to give him a hug. He continued to sob very sadly. I don't remember either of us saying anything. I just held him in the dark room while he cried. I felt so bad for him, but I didn't know what to do.

"I want to come apart and dig myself a little hole, 'cause it's always raining in my head."

— Staind, *Epiphany*

Chapter 26:

RAIN

I listened to Staind's "Epiphany" over and over, sitting alone in my car one night in Garden of the Gods Park, on a hill overlooking the lights of Colorado Springs. I cried as I listened. It wasn't just that the powerful, dreadful words and the anguished voice reminded me of Graham. It was that Graham had left this CD in my car and I'd discovered it several days after his death. All I could imagine was him listening to it in the last few days of his life.

Graham had a broad taste in music, everything from Mahler to Stevie Ray Vaughn to Neil Young to Ozzy Osborne. Much of the music we shared an appreciation for, but there were bands and genres I had little-to-no familiarity with, like a band whose name has stuck with me because it seemed to epitomize Graham's dark side: Burning Witch. I remember the band only because I keep running into a photo of Graham dated December 10, 2004, in which he is wearing a black T-shirt with a caricature of a skeleton cloaked in long, flaming garb below the words "Burning Witch."

Graham is looking straight at the camera, forlorn and sad, although you can't see his eyes because he is wearing dark Ray-Ban sunglasses. Wisps of blond hair escape from his ponytail and cover his face. The image is of a solemn, yet beautiful, young man.

He was a beautiful soul living in a body wracked day after day, night after night, by severe headaches, sleeplessness followed by long bouts of deep sleep, and, above all, depression. It was his double misfortune to have a dreadful disease that few understood and that no one, least of all Graham, could seem to remedy.

It wasn't always like that. As a young child, Graham could not have been happier and more engaged with the world around him. He was quick to learn, quick to pick up sports, quick to take a fancy to the arts, such as music and movies, and just generally a very eager, earnest, and contented young boy.

Then, in third or fourth grade, we noticed a change beginning in him. He would tell us—especially his mother—that he was "scared" and "sad," and at times had spells in which he would cry and say he didn't feel well. One day, Mary entered Graham's room to find him jumping up and down on his bed like a trampoline, showing her how anxious he was and telling her how sad he felt.

Alarmed, we took him to a child psychiatrist in Denver, who began seeing him on a regular basis. Mary would load up the four boys and travel the hour to Denver so Graham could have sessions with this doctor, which seemed to help him overall. This began an ongoing process of therapy that would continue for the rest of his life. We switched at some point to a doctor in Colorado Springs, and then switched to someone else after that. I remember many sessions in which Mary and I met with Graham and his doctor and discussed his progress. There seemed to be some progress, but Graham's depression held on and never seemed to go away entirely. As he entered middle school, it got worse. And by high school, he was not only dealing with a seemingly treatment-resistant depression, but also complained regularly of headaches, stomach aches, heartburn, sleep disorder, and general anxiety.

It was an awful thing to witness as parents, and it made us feel hopeless and ineffective. We tried as hard as we could to help, but it never seemed to be enough.

From the beginning, I was frustrated by my incomprehension of Graham's experience. Though I had seen his mother struggle most of her adult life with this disease, I had not been able to understand or even really accept the devastating power of depression.

It didn't help that our society generally is very reluctant to even acknowledge depression as a disease to be treated, and prefers to see this malady as a personal trait to be muscled into submission by the victim. I found my own understanding of the disease often confused. I was plagued by the idea that depression was perhaps simply a mood or behavior caused and controlled by the individual or his family. Was there really a physiological basis? Maybe these symptoms of sadness and hopelessness *were* the result of a character flaw, a personal shortcoming, a parental inconsistency?

But the more I read about depression and the more I listened to Graham's doctors and others who knew this disease, I became certain that though one's personality and environment can provide triggers, the real cause of this disease can be traced to the hard-wiring, the cellular structure, and the biochemistry of the brain. As people study the disease, the myths are beginning to fall away, and there's a growing consensus in the medical and scientific communities that depressed people experience very specific neurological, chemical and biological abnormalities and deficiencies. The cells of certain mood-regulating parts of the brain become much less resilient and less healthy overall in a depressed person than in a healthy person. Though its exact causes remain unknown, this disease does real and devastating damage to the brain and its ability to function normally.

One of the problems with depression is that you can't see it. All the disorder and dysfunction goes on in the domain of the brain and its elaborate systems of communication and control. Except for that forlorn expression on a face in a photograph, the depressed person looks healthy. There is no apparent wound, no visible injury, no physical mark of disease. What you can see are the symptoms. The drowsiness, the distraction, and the detachment are there, but the causes of those symptoms are concealed, hidden deeply in the skull.

In these modern times, what we as laymen, scientists, and doctors know about depression is rapidly expanding. A therapist told me recently that it wouldn't be long until there are inhalers for the depressed, just as there are inhalers for sufferers of asthma. The medication will go directly to the root of the problem that creates such terrible suffering, swiftly and certainly.

The University of Michigan Depression Center, which has an individual memorial fund and plaque in memory of Graham because of all the contributions in his name, continually announces breakthroughs in both the study and treatment of depression. In a recent bulletin, the center announced a new transcranial magnetic stimulation treatment for patients who are either resistant to more traditional treatments or who cannot tolerate the sometimes-awful side effects of medication, a category that I believe would describe Graham. This brand-new form of treatment uses magnetic coils to induce modest electrical activity in the brain.

But for Graham, all that is too late. What he suffered, he suffered with all too little help from the world of science or medicine.

I think one of the demons that most haunted him was his acute self-awareness. From a very early age he keenly felt his relationship to the outside world, in all its beauty and brutality. He knew how events and people made him feel, and he knew these feelings relentlessly tormented him, long after the event or the person was gone. He was also very aware of his shortcomings, the same shortcomings we all have, especially growing up. With Graham, these normal problems and inabilities became something larger, something more onerous. He was hard on himself. It was difficult for him to accept himself against his standard of perfection.

I really think these issues were caused by his depression, that he physically did not have the capacity to deal with the stresses and problems of life the way most of us do. Those of us who are not suffering from depression will never fully understand this.

In the months following Graham's death, I increased my efforts to find out more about depression. I had always had a bitter and nagging interest

"For in the middle of the journey of life I found myself in a dark wood, for I had lost the right path."

– Dante, *Inferno*

Chapter 27:
AGAINST DEPRESSION

in the subject, because Mary and some of her family members had been lifelong sufferers of the disease.

Maybe Graham had had the genetic makings of depression from the womb—something I'd always wondered. Maybe he never really had a decent chance at a healthy life. Or maybe depression was more situational in nature, meaning that certain life stresses caused damage and created depression. Perhaps certain personal shortcomings I'd passed on to Graham had created this perplexing situation: my early extreme shyness, my inability to express myself and my emotions, and my propensity to hide myself from the outside world because I feared rejection. Maybe I'd also passed on to him the sweeping headaches that would strike me unannounced. I had had time to grow out of these traits, but my son had not.

The current thinking on depression was best summed up for me in a book called *Against Depression*, by Dr. Peter Kramer. This professor of psychiatry is also the author of *Listening to Prozac*, a popular book released in 1993 that brought to the general public a new understanding of depression. Dr. Kramer found through research that the changes in brain chemistry brought about by Prozac have a wide variety of effects, often giving users greater feelings of self-worth and confidence, less sensitivity to social rejection, and even a greater willingness to take risks. He cites cases of mildly depressed patients who took the drug and not only felt better, but underwent remarkable personality transformations. He found this disconcerting, and questioned whether the medicated or unmedicated version was the person's "real" self.

While we all can intellectually debate the "real" self, what Dr. Kramer solidified was the fact that depression is indeed a medically based disease, and a drug like Prozac can in fact lift the veil of depression and alleviate the illness.

In his book, published the year Graham died, Dr. Kramer launched an all-out assault on the myths surrounding depression. Depression is not a "heroic melancholy" or romantic affliction, as Western culture has long believed. Rather, Dr. Kramer asserted, depression is clearly a disease, the science of which he explains in medical detail, and one that has a biological, not philosophical, source.

After covering antidepressant drugs, Dr. Kramer seemed to be looking squarely at the disease itself in this book, which I found both helpful and distressing. It clarified to an extent what had been happening inside my son, saddening but also enlightening me.

This was a disease that could be triggered by many causes, but at its base was enabled by the brain's cellular and chemical makeup. The same trauma, or stress that triggers depression in one brain would not cause depression in another, healthier brain. And depressed brains cannot recover from stress or trauma in the same way as healthy brains, Dr. Kramer concluded.

This well-informed scientist was telling me things that made Graham's plight clearer. His research clearly showed how depression endangers nerve cells, disrupts brain functioning, and damages the heart and blood vessels, all the while increasingly altering personal perspective and judgment and interfering with parenting and family life. The problem with depression is that these were very new findings, and the disease has long been misunderstood and wrongly portrayed, so many people still firmly view depression as a personal weakness or character flaw, not a medical disease.

Even worse, Kramer explains, depression has often been glorified, linked in our culture to a long tradition of "heroic melancholy," which was understood as an ennobling source of creativity, integrity, insight, and sensuality, and even as a form of courage; as an awareness of the absurd, chaotic, and brief nature of our lives. Tracing these beliefs from Aristotle to the Romantics to Picasso, and to the present-day memoirs of mood disorder, Kramer suggests that the pervasiveness of the illness has distorted our impression of what it is to be human. He shows how a head-on look at the truth of depression will change our sense of self, our tastes in art and in love, and our accounts of what it is to live a good life.

Dr. Kramer's book also tries to unravel the interconnectedness of the dark mood and the reflective soul, a mixture that seems to represent many creative people, including my own son. In the world of artists and intellectuals, many think that pain equals genius, while lack of pain equals lack of depth.

This delusion, this misunderstanding of creativity, needs to stop, Dr. Kramer argues. Depression is a disease, plain and simple, that needs to be treated wholeheartedly as such.

It is this "cult of melancholy," as Dr. Kramer refers to it, that Graham seemed to dwell in all too often. It was as if he was drawn into a world where others suffered. I could see this in the music that he began listening to, in the books he began reading, and in the people he began hanging out with.

My happy little child, the one whose smile and bright eyes you can see so clearly in all those early family pictures, had changed. The innocence and happiness of youth had waned.

"Everything passes away—suffering, pain, blood, hunger, pestilence. The sword will pass away too, but the stars will remain when the shadows of our presence and our deeds have vanished from earth. There is no man who does not know that. Why, then, will we not turn our eyes toward the stars? Why?"
– Mikhail Bulgakov, *The White Guard*

Chapter 28:

BLACK DOGS AND NOONDAY DEMONS

Writers have been writing about depression and its earlier term, melancholy, for centuries. Before Graham's death and since, I have read my share.

The most poignant and succinct personal account of depression I've found is William Styron's *Darkness Visible: A Memoir of Madness*. The author of *Sophie's Choice* and other intense books, Styron gives a clear, succinct description of his personal experience with a bout of depression. Styron also discusses the same romanticized notion of depression found in arts and literature that irritates Dr. Kramer, calling it the "desolation of melancholia."

But he admits, "To most of those who have experienced it, the horror of depression is so overwhelming as to be quite beyond expression, hence the frustrated sense of inadequacy found in the work of even the greatest artists."

Though Styron was an extremely accomplished, Pulitzer Prize-winning writer himself, he found "self-loathing" to be depresssion's "premier badge."

Even the label "depression" is problematic, according to Styron: "When I was first aware that I had been laid low by the disease, I felt the need, among other things, to register a strong protest against the word 'depression.'" Its traditional term, "melancholia," was also insufficient to describe what he was suffering, but the word "depression" had "a bland tonality, lacking any magisterial presence, used indifferently to describe an economic decline or a rut in the ground, a true wimp of a word for such a major illness."

He eventually was hospitalized for seven weeks after making his own secret arrangements to commit suicide—a death he referred to as "moving into the abyss." At the time of his greatest despair, he said, it was his only salvation.

Through his hospitalization and a long series of medications, most of which didn't work, Styron recovered. "For me the real healers were seclusion and time," he writes.

Other literate sufferers of depression have added their perspectives, which I found as I scoured the intellectual landscape for more information on what my son experienced and what I might have missed in watching his suffering.

In the essay "A Journey Through Darkness," published in *New York Times Sunday Magazine* on May 6, 2009, Daphne Merkin wrote that her depression came early and still lurked four decades later, despite repeated treatment and frequent hospitalization. She wrote, "It is an affliction that often starts young and goes unheeded—younger than would seem possible, as if in exiting the womb I was enveloped in a gray and itchy wool blanket instead of a soft, pastel-colored bunting."

Her story ends with a flicker of hope for her future, albeit a temporary one. After extensive treatment and time, Ms. Merkin saw her depression lift. "I knew for certain it would return," she wrote, "sneaking up on me when I wasn't looking, but meanwhile there were bound to be glimpses of light if only I stayed around and held fast to the long perspective. It was a chance that seemed worth taking."

Before modern medicine knew much about mental illnesses, French writer and philosopher Albert Camus described what most certainly was depression as his "most unsettling pessimism" that transformed the world for him into a meaningless experience. "There is an existential dread and purposelessness that seems to be lurking under the surface every day and night, but that most of us are healthy enough to avoid being pulled down by," he commented. Now we know that he was not at fault; victims of depression cannot avoid this dread, but they can seek treatment.

Les Murray, an Australian poet, tells of his lifetime of suffering panic attacks and depressive episodes in a book he called Killing the Black Dog, a title he later regretted. "I know now that you can't kill the Dog," he wrote in 2009 in a new afterward to his earlier book. "And that thus my earlier account has the wrong title: it should be called Learning the Black Dog."

"What I still do mourn is the terrible waste of energy the Dog has exacted from me, over my lifetime and especially in my twenty horror years," he concluded. "And how much more I might have achieved if I'd owned a single, healthy mind working on my side."

Unlike others who were confronted continually with depression, Murray said he never contemplated suicide but he remembered "good friends who had gone that way." One friend in particular he remembered looking "to a fresh start in Heaven. I'll never blame her, and if you do, you've never been where she and I have been and you can't say anything meaningful to us or about us."

Andrew Solomon declared in the first words of his book on depression that the disease was a "flaw in love. To be creatures who love, we must be creatures who can despair at what we lose, and depression is the mechanism of that despair." Solomon's book is a rather complete and impressive account of depression in which he describes his own bouts with the disease with the stories of others along with an exhaustive account of the scientific, philosophical, historical, political and cultural aspects surrounding depression. His book is called *The Noonday Demon, an Atlas of Depression."*

At the end of his book, Solomon finds reason for hope. "The opposite of depression is not happiness but vitality, and my life, as I write this, is vital, even when sad."

It's the same hopeful uptick Dr. Ghaemi, the Tufts University professor of psychiatry, noted in his book on depressive leaders. "Their weakness is the secret to their strength."

"What about all the people living the nightmare hurt? That won't go away no matter how hard they try. They've got to pay time and time again, time and time again."

– Van Morrison, *Ancient Highway*

Chapter 29:

A FATHER'S LAMENT

I'm not one to normally second-guess my past actions. I believe in the power of forgiving myself and moving on, using mistakes as reminders, not punishment. *Don't hold onto it*, I often urge myself, *let it go*. Simply move on and learn from your mistake, do better next time. Now that something truly horrible had happened to me, I couldn't apply the same principles that had allowed me to live through my days—and sleep through my nights—unencumbered by the past.

Despite clear deficiencies in my personality, I have been self-assured, independent, and easygoing most of my life. The tragedy of Graham's death changed that orientation, tilting it away from certainty and toward doubt.

I noticed, with the help of my therapist, that my thoughts went through a constant sorting process, searching for answers that couldn't be found. It was as if there was a micro-flashlight constantly sweeping around inside my skull. Any illumination that came was fleeting and confusing. The emotions that were lit were often sad and empty. There were misconceptions and misperceptions that I didn't want to deal with, because they provided bad information, bad thoughts and feelings. I wanted to know what the truth was and deal with that, not wallow around in lies or untruths.

Perhaps that was why I wrote so much, to aid the searching process with a tool I'm comfortable with. The act of typing words on my keyboard seemed to bring clarity to what I was thinking and feeling, slow and painful though the process could be. I found myself compelled to get my thoughts down in written words, as if it were the only way I'd ever understand them. I typed in my electronic journal, scribbled in countless journals, and even tapped out notes on my phone as I was stopped at a traffic light. Why was I driven to do this? Was I documenting my grief? Was I searching for something I thought was there which I hadn't yet found? Was it my continued attempt to stay connected to Graham? Was it a feeble attempt to flee from my grief, to avoid addressing it head on? I didn't know, so I kept writing.

I still have questions. Was I a good father to Graham? Why did he die? What could I have done to prevent this? Did he have a good life while he was alive? Was he dealing with a disease that was unbearable? Should I have helped him more to rid himself of that disease? What will be the continuing effect of his death on my family's life? What kind of person am I? What kind of family are we? Where did he go? Does he have a spirit that lives on though his body does not? If so, where is that spirit?

In the years following Graham's death, I constantly sought answers to these questions, knowing full well some might not have answers, at least not that I would find in my lifetime and within the limits of my own mind. There must be *some* answers for me. I felt I must find them so I could have some peace. I felt there are many perceptions of the truth, but stripped of all perceptions, there is but one truth, one way things actually happened, second by second, minute by minute, one existential truth that reflects the reality of how things unfolded. That truth is what I wanted to know and feared I couldn't know.

For example, I will never know exactly how Graham felt about a lot of things as his life unfolded. Even if he were alive today and I asked him about how he felt or perceived a specific incident in his life, his words could never adequately explain how he felt. There was the reality of what went on inside him at the time, but maybe he wouldn't even recall it. Every moment of his life had its own reality of feeling or thought. As close as I can get to knowing that, the better off I am, I think. But I still know that I can never fully get to where I want to be, because I am another human being. I am his father. I cared as deeply about what he was thinking and feeling and experiencing as is possible for a human to care. Still, I cannot get close enough to what he experienced.

Everything is so relative and so messy. One day, running along a dirt road in the mountains, I looked up from the road and saw the trees ahead were covered with orange, dead pine needles, a picture of discouragement, disappointment, disease, and even death. It was a bleak sight, and it affected my mood immediately. Then I glanced upward and saw in the distance the beautiful mountain peaks, bright with perfect, white snow and grand against the blue sky. It seemed I had the choice on what I focused on as I trudged through this life: the disease and death of the near, or the overall beauty of the whole. Both are real. Both are part of nature. Neither can be denied or eliminated. But with a momentary movement of my eyes, I could change my view of the world and my internal landscape. It seemed I had a choice, then, to focus on one thing that is beautiful or one thing that is not. I had that choice—I still do—and I must choose one or the other, because my mind's eye can only focus on one thing at a time.

It also occurred to me at times that I was missing the point altogether in how I dealt with the death of my son. It wasn't my intellectual or sensory focus that mattered, but the feelings I had. This was, and is, a harder task for me. This is not how I am wired. This is not how I was raised. This is not the easiest way for me to try to understand the world around me.

I like to think of myself as a proficient problem solver, fixing what is wrong around me, or even within me. But since February 18, 2005, I've had a problem that can't be solved, no matter how hard I try.

"Hanging on in quiet desperation...time is gone, the song is over, thought I'd have something more to say."

–Pink Floyd, *Time*

Chapter 30:

HELPING HANDS

The year after Graham's death is but a horrible haze in my mind. I was living in a surreal world, where nothing seemed the same as it was before February 18, 2005. So many of my friends and family reached out to me to help pull me from the haze, but I barely remember what they said or what they did. I was so grief-stricken and so confused; I don't know how I survived. But I did and I continued to go on with my life. Step by step, day by day.

On the first anniversary of Graham's death our family of five assembled in our living room in our Monument home in a sorrowful and awkward attempt do something to "commemorate" the day. I read a poem I had written earlier in the day:

A Year

As the sun sets, it is a year
Since our Graham has gone.

And a year and nearly a day of feeling
The worst pain I have ever felt.
I'm overwhelmed and confused,
I don't know where to turn or look
To find my Graham or to make it okay
Because Graham's not here and it is not okay.
There are days I can see a way to push ahead,
To remember and love and feel Graham
But to live the rest of my life somehow
And perhaps come to terms with what has happened.
Those are only fleeting, taunting moments
That come in a whirl and leave in haste
Leaving me with my sadness, staring at the meaninglessness
That seems to be the guardian of this world.
And as the sun sets on this solemn day,
The veil of blackness rises from the earth to the heavens
Bringing yet more darkness, sadness, and tears
But also bringing the sparkle of the stars to my hazy eyes.

Then, a few weeks later, alone in a hotel room on a business trip, I complained to myself:

I can't cry
I try
But can't
I feel it in my head
But I can't cry
Sometimes
My chest heaves
and my head wrenches
But there are no tears
I can't cry

Still later that same year, on a trip to Mexico with friends, when I should have been relaxed and having fun, I couldn't do either. I was restless, my sadness turning to madness:

   Let it be
   I can no longer pretend
   That I'm anywhere else
   But here, in the madness
   Of what this life presents
   To me and all
   Nothingness at all
   When you look below the stone
   There appear to be
   Things you recognize
   And things you know
   But they are not really there
   At least as they appear
   They are nothing at all
   Like all the rest
   Or if they appear
   Don't believe what you see
   It is nothing but an illusion
   A magician's trick performed
   Before your eyes.
   Fill the pages with words
   If that is what you want to do
   But don't be deceived
   That it means something
   Or is different than others' words
   Because you see nothing that
   Someone else has not seen
   And believed as true, but is not.
   As the sky clouds
   And then clears
   What has that done to help?
   You understand the real nature

Of what is nature?
You see the clouds, you see the blue
But in a matter of time
They are gone, never to repeat
As it was just then, just now
Never will it be the same
Never will it be as it is now
But the madness, indeed,
Will remain with you.

One of my friends asked me during this time if I was angry. I remember looking at him and thinking about why he was asking me that, if I seemed angry. Very rarely did I feel anger that I can remember, but I do remember the sadness. Not a day went by that I didn't have at least a few moments in which I felt so sad that I could not begin to express what it feels like. It is deep and awful and more. I have cried, while hiking in the woods, or walking outside before going to bed and whispering goodnight to my son while looking at the night sky, or while stopped in my car listening to a song that reminds me of Graham. It's just that I don't cry often, fewer times by far than I'm sad, and I usually cry alone.

Most people are understandably reluctant to ask someone about a loss like mine. But when they do, it is helpful because it is acknowledgement, confirmation. I never go into any detail when the conversations come up, because it is hard for me and I know the person asking really doesn't want to make me feel worse and is probably quite uncomfortable with talking about death. "People just don't talk about death, do they," my son Seth once said. I had to agree with him.

I have close friends who allow and even encourage me to talk about my loss, but, guys being guys, it's usually a short conversation. They are more comfortable doing something with me; they prefer to just be with me and not really have to talk about it.

"Let's go for a hike," one friend offered.

"Let's take a road trip," another suggested.

"Let's climb a mountain sometime soon," another proposed. They're showing me they are thinking of me, and they are tender and helpful.

To show his sympathy for Mary and me, and to show his love for Graham, one of my dear friends and running buddies over the years, Jim Latchaw, announced he was going to run the Pikes Peak Marathon in Graham's name. We were touched. At the end of the race, he received a fleece jacket with the marathon logo embossed on the front. He gave the jacket to Mary, who held it to her chest with tears in her eyes. On the front of the jacket, embroidered below the race logo, were the words:

In Memory of Graham Winter Stingley

Jim watched Graham grow up and always had a smile and kind words for him. Jim, who ran a surveying company with his wife, Mary, told me once when we were running, "I should have hired Graham to do surveying for me. He was a smart kid. He was a good kid." Then, with downcast eyes, he added, "I should have helped him."

Then there was Jerry Mahoney. We met in Omaha when we both worked for the newspaper there in the early 1980s. His son, Michael, died unexpectedly and suddenly as a student in New York several years before Graham died. We didn't stay in touch after I left Nebraska for Colorado in 1985, and, though he lived briefly in Colorado Springs as well, he ended up in Austin, Texas.

After Graham's death, another friend suggested I call Jerry. From our first phone conversation on, we had a bond that I've experienced with no other male friend. He could understand. I could understand. There was nothing we could not ask or say to each other. It was a very critical and important relationship for me from the first time we talked.

We kept a steady flow of e-mail correspondence. We would expound on everything from our gut feelings about our losses to our philosophies about what lay after death. We would lament what we had and hadn't done when our sons were alive, and discuss with some dread what we saw as our human shortcomings since they'd died. He was always kind enough to check in periodically with me just to see how I was doing. On one such occasion, I had just taken a solo day hike to a lake high up in the Rockies not too far from my home. I wrote back to him:

Jerry:

I'm not sure I can describe how I feel on occasions like two days ago on my hike. It is as if there is this tremendous, overpowering sadness deep within me that is too much for me to handle. Sometimes I even think of dying myself, right there on the trail. It's not that I want to "join" Graham in some kind of afterlife, but that the sadness is too much to bear. And maybe I do just want to "be with" Graham. Of course, I always think about my boys and Mary and that gives me a clear reason not to die. I then think that I'm going to die someday anyway, so why rush it.

I spend some time thinking about how Graham just disappeared, that he is nothing now but a bunch of ashes sitting in a cabinet in our living room. I can't understand what happened to him and how all of a sudden he could be so absolutely gone. He is nowhere to be seen or touched or talked to. Of course while I'm walking in the woods I often remember the times I spent with Graham outdoors, which was considerable. He especially liked the deep, dark forest, with tall trees that made the forest floor dark and lonely, which fit his mood most of the time. Also, on camping trips he would sleep very late, and I would go take a run or hike on my own, but know he was back at camp sleeping, avoiding his depression.

As I hike, I have the chance to think clearly, especially coming back down the mountain, when I don't have to exert myself and can just walk through the woods in a trancelike state, letting my mind wander, but a clear wander. I was thinking about all the things I can no longer share with Graham now that he is gone, like new music I have discovered or books I have read or ideas I have pondered. That makes me incredibly sad because he was such a deep person and always understood what I was saying and was so keenly aware what I was thinking about life. We had this deep, philosophical connection, although we were very different in many ways, largely due to our age difference. We could walk through the mountains, too, together and not talking, and know that each of us was enjoying that moment immensely. He understood and appreciated the power of nature in much the same way I do.

But I became the saddest when I remembered a time when I was a young father and took the boys camping. The four of them were a handful, and once I lost my temper, grabbed Graham by the coat, and reprimanded him for something. I was thinking what kind of trauma that would have caused his young mind—he was perhaps eight or ten. I think I picked on him more because he was the oldest. I cried on the trail thinking of that incident, and asked Graham out loud to forgive me. It was just part of a larger feeling that Graham had a sad life and a hard life, and maybe I was a part of the reason. Maybe deep down I was not a good father to him, at least not good enough to help him be happy, and that eventually led him to his early death. Then there is this sort of nothingness feeling that overcomes me sometimes, in which I just feel numb to the whole fucked-up world, because my son is gone and nothing else really matters. I feel dulled, like I don't really understand anything, especially what happened to my son. I can especially feel that in the woods, where everything is quiet and there is "nothing" in the midst of "everything." There are great stands of trees just waiting to die. There were also many trees stricken by fire or beetle kill, and these huge black or grey trunks stood up tall but dead. I thought quite a bit about how all this live stuff is only going to die and that I'm just a part of this whole-natural-life-and-then-death cycle, and I don't really want to be. As Becker calls it, our "creatureliness," or something to that effect. And Graham was part of that cycle of life but died prematurely and did not have the full and ripe life that most animals and plants have—he didn't even get a chance to live out the relatively short life that humans are allotted. He was a young tree struck early by beetles. Anyway, those were some of my thoughts as I hiked the other day. Thanks for asking, my friend.

—Steven

"You will always be a slave to the quiet darkness of your memories...and that's the truth my friend, the ugly truth. I got proof, my friend."
– Lucinda Williams, *The Ugly Truth*

Chapter 31:

THE MAN ON THE SIDEWALK

In addition to the support I received from friends, a class in creative nonfiction writing I took at the University of Colorado–Boulder, where my three sons were attending school at the time, also helped me. As we introduced ourselves the first night of class, the teacher asked us why we wanted to take the class, and I remember boldly saying I wanted to write about losing my son. I also met a woman in the class who would later invite me to her writing group, which I found both helpful and fascinating.

I wrote several essays for the class, all about different aspects of my life. This came easily to me because I was writing a personal column for the local paper at the time and I had always enjoyed writing about various topics. But what I really wanted to write about was Graham. Finally, in my last essay for the class, I got the courage to write about what was really on my mind. I wrote about something that had just happened to me. I called the essay "The Man on the Sidewalk."

I saw the man walking down the Sixteenth Street Mall in downtown

Denver. His back was to me, and his long hair fell past his shoulders. He had on long, awkward-looking shorts that went below his knees, and some sort of large jacket whose color clashed with his shorts. He wore basketball shoes.

The sight of this young man from behind stopped me. I merely stood on the sidewalk, watching him walk away from me down the busy sidewalk. He was alone. I wondered where he was going and who he was.

I never really saw his face. I didn't want to. I watched as he walked away and disappeared. I was left shaken, thinking about the last time I'd seen Graham, who looked so similar to this man. It was on this same street, over three years ago, that Graham had walked away from me with his long hair and awkward shorts and then disappeared.

These things pop up from time to time. It's not that I need to be reminded that he is gone. I think about it every day. But then there are times when it seems more real, more awful, more certain.

And most of the time, it's not as if I'm immediately saddened. It is more of a deep, empty feeling than anything else. I don't cry. I don't break down and wail in grief, like I do sometimes in dreams. I just keep going, walking away on the sidewalk or driving down the road, with my deep, empty feeling.

Beliefs might make things easier. Maybe that man on that street was Graham in some new, reincarnated form. Maybe some almighty God placed him there, ten feet in front of me, on a street I rarely walk. Maybe this man on this street was sent by Graham to give me some comfort or connection with his far-away soul.

But no, I don't have those beliefs, so they can't help. All I have is rational reality. A young man dies and he is dead. He is gone forever from me. There is no alternative to this line of reasoning. People can believe what they want, but it doesn't mean a lick to me. My son is simply gone.

That doesn't mean I can't picture or "see" my son, or his "spirit," if you *must put it that way. In some ways, he is as real today as he ever was. I won't forget the things that he did or the person he was. I won't forget the hurt he suffered or his wit and intellect. I still can see him sleeping on the couch or smiling in the passenger seat next to me. Those things are still very real.*

When I do cry, it is usually only in my dreams, as I have said. Then it's a deep, awful sobbing. Last night I dreamt that I was bent over in the corner of a small restaurant, crying quietly to myself so no one knew. But I could hear the muffled talk of people behind me, expressing concern about me, and some people saying that I was sad because I had lost my son and that I blamed myself.

By the light of day, I don't normally blame myself. Thank goodness for that. But there must be some part of me that feels guilt. Some part that comes out when my ability to rationalize is asleep and my mind is free to feel whatever it may. Then I blame myself, and it hurts.

After all, what is a father's main job? It is to keep his son safe from harm, and in that respect I failed as a father. You can spend some time figuring out how that isn't really the way to think about it, but the results speak for themselves, don't they? I am the father. He was the son. I am still alive, and he isn't. It is pretty clear what happened here.

I used to see Graham and talk to him in my dreams in the months after he died. It was wonderful to see him and to think that he in fact was not dead, but still alive. It was such a relief. I was so happy.

But of course the dream would end with him walking away, or driving away in the backseat of a car, and he would be gone and I would wake and realize it was not real; that the only real thing was that he was gone.

I'm still trying slowly and desperately to make sense of what has happened. And I can't. I'm still trying to "move on" and enjoy my life to the extent that's possible. And I can't. I'm still trying to understand what my son experienced when he was alive and why he died at such a young age. And I can't.

"Finally, the lessons of impermanence taught me this: loss constitutes an odd kind of fullness; despair empties out into an unquenchable appetite for life."
— Gretel Ehrlich, *The Solace of Open Spaces*

Chapter 32:

VISIONS AND DREAMS

In the meantime, I remained haunted by visions during the day and by dreams at night.

In early December 2008, I went for a run after work in a mountain park near my office. The air was cold but clear, the sky cloudless and deep blue. I ran on the icy, rocky trail, watching every step so I didn't slip or stumble. Running free and alone in the foothills of the mountains felt good, as it has these many years. As my body took over, I began to relax and focus. The mental rushing slowed, and the unimportant melted away.

As I came to the top of a mesa in the park, I turned off the trail so I could stop, catch my breath, and look around on a broad, flat rock. I had been alone since the beginning of my run more than a half hour earlier, and now I stood there by myself in the silence.

I looked west toward downtown Colorado Springs, which always looks beautiful against the broad expanse of Pikes Peak. But the sun was setting and it was too bright to look in that direction. So I turned away from the sun in the west and looked to the east, where I was struck by a beautiful, rising full moon.

As always, this sight connected me with Graham. Whenever I glimpse the moon, in the evening, late at night, or even sometimes in the day, I invariably think of him. I don't need a physical prompt to think of my lost son, but the moon always brings my thoughts to him.

Now, standing at the edge of this mesa, I talked to my son sadly as my eyes fixed on the moon. I greeted him. I told him I missed him. I told him I loved him.

Then, oddly, as I'd never done before, I asked Graham to go running with me. I began to slowly run down the trail and imagined Graham jogging behind me at first, then ahead of me, since he could run faster than I could. He was happy. He was smiling. He was loping like a buck down the trail, and we were enjoying this nice moment on this quiet, snowy mesa, with the sun setting to our left and the moon rising on our right. The clear, cold air invigorated us as we ran down the path, and we were happy together; very happy together.

Then there were the dreams. They often provided me with a way to reconnect with my son, at least by night. By day, they changed nothing.

In one of those dreams, I saw a two-year-old Graham. I walked into a room that seemed like a giant nursery, perhaps even in a hospital setting. Though filled with beds, this very large room held only two people. One was a young man in his early twenties, who seemed to be in charge and was cleaning up and organizing the room. When I asked about Graham, he smiled and said he was doing very well and some other sincere but well-practiced niceties.

He pointed to a far side of the room, where Graham was in a crib-like bed on the floor. To see him, I had to lean on another, larger bed, covered with a white sheet; everything was white in the room. I leaned over the bed, on my stomach, and could see Graham down below. He was playing happily by himself. He was beautiful and smiling. He looked up at me and said, "Hello, Daddy," and I said hello to him and touched his face, his right cheek. His skin was white, clear and soft. I began to cry because I loved and missed him so much, and he was so beautiful and happy. He said, "Why are you crying, Daddy?" and I said, "I just love seeing you." And he said, "Don't cry, Daddy."

Then there are the dreams in which I go back to times when our boys were younger—and all alive. These are wonderful dreams where I am living in a moment where everything is just perfect, the boys are happy and playing and enjoying being with each other and myself, often with Mary there as well. One such vivid and beautiful dream happened at a rock quarry, like the kind where Mary and I would swim in the Kansas countryside. The water was clear and cool, and the boys were jumping off the rock sides into the deep water. They were all young boys, younger than their teens, when pure innocence and enjoyment enveloped us all.

I sat at the edge of the water, up a few feet on the hard brown rock of the quarry, watching as the boys swam around in the water, then climbed out and heaved their wet little bodies back into the water. They would momentarily disappear into the dark blue of the deeper water as they splashed down and sank. Then they would pop back up, their smiling faces emerging from the liquid surface.

They were happy. They were alive.

And then there are my nightmares, the indescribable ones in which my son Graham dies.

"O, my child, what cozier nest, for rosier rest could love have found you? Sleep baby dear, sleep without fear. Mother's two arms are clasped around you, mother is here with you forever."

– Alfred Graves, *Irish Lullaby*

Chapter 33:

A BABY IN AUGUST

It was the morning that changed my life, perhaps more than any other. Very early—it must have been three o'clock—Mary woke up, saying she was having strong contractions and she was ready to give birth to our first child. We scrambled to get ready to leave for the hospital in the cool dark of the summer night and soon were driving as quickly as we could down the empty streets of Omaha. We were headed to Methodist Hospital in the middle of the city, some ten miles or so from our rented home in the hills north of Omaha.

I remember vividly driving south on 60th Street. The wide boulevard was eerily vacant and silent. The disorientation of rising so unexpectedly from bed in the middle of the night and the anxious anticipation made the world seem unreal, as if we were caught together in an extended dream. The air felt strangely cool as it flowed in the car's open window, a pleasant respite from Nebraska's August heat. We talked little on our ride to the hospital. I don't think we knew what to say to each other.

It was August 7, 1981, and Graham was about to be born.

Trying to recount the rest of the morning is difficult now, more than two decades later. There was the trauma and then joy of the birthing process, which Mary experienced firsthand, with me as a wide-eyed spectator. I stopped being the spectator once the tiny, fleshy baby boy was born. I could then see him and hold him. That is when my life changed.

I had never been particularly interested in children. This is probably because, up to that point, I had spent most of my life being one. I hadn't envisioned myself as a father. When I looked to my future, I dreamed of careers and roles that would change the world. I was going to be someone special, someone who would write the words or ask the questions that would make a difference. I saw myself as a big-picture guy with big things to accomplish.

Then Graham was born. It was 3:15 p.m. August 7, 1981. The instant fatherhood took me by surprise. I loved it from the start. For some reason, a memory of his birth that's stuck with me is of walking across the street from the hospital to a McDonald's restaurant to get a late lunch. It was the first time I'd been out of the hospital since we had rushed in earlier in the morning. The sun was now up and shining very brightly, rapidly creating the heat of another August day. There were a few people in the restaurant, but they seemed so apart from me and my new life, given what had just happened.

I felt different. It was as if Graham's birth had changed my sense of self. I could feel it in my mind and my body. I had a new, special energy, an energy I would continue to feel for the rest of my life in one way or another. As I stepped up to the metal counter and ordered my lunch, I felt like announcing to the unknowing clerk, "I am a father."

The feeling of elation continued. In the first few weeks after we brought this tiny baby home from the hospital, the routine of our lives altered to fit his needs, especially for Mary, but for me as well. Mary would get up in the middle of the night to reach over and lift tiny Graham up out of the wicker basket where he spent his nights next to our bed, and bring him to her breast to nurse him. I don't think I've seen a more pure and lovely sight in my life. We created a nursery for him in one of the tiny bedrooms of our house, and suddenly it was the center of our world, full of life.

It was a grand situation, a thrilling time like none else except the birth of Graham's three younger brothers over the next five years.

In these early months, a nurse from Mary's postnatal doctor's office came by our home for routine checkups on Graham's health and progress. Like many expectant parents, I had serious fears during Mary's pregnancy that things would not be well. This life that was forming within Mary was unseen. No one could predict with any certainty that this baby would be whole and healthy when it was born. I feared the worst. What if this life we were responsible for creating was sick with a disease, was not the complete and perfect being it deserved to be? I was extremely relieved when Graham was born and everything appeared just right.

Then, on one of her visits, the nurse expressed concern that Graham's soft spot, or fontanel, was missing. I remember watching her feeling the top of Graham's tiny skull as he lay on the top of a dresser converted into a changing table in his little nursery, decorated in bright, cheerful blues and yellows. This might not present a problem for our baby, she reassured us, but it was something to watch. When she came back, she would check it again. Worst case, this malady, called craniosynostosis, could cause problems later in life, including seizures and even death, she warned.

Despite my earlier fears, Mary and I were shocked. How could this beautiful, seemingly perfect little baby have something wrong with him? That was unthinkable. It was the first time in our lives that we truly faced the fear that our own child could be sick, injured, or otherwise affected by something outside our control. I had always had the luxury of a healthy family; no one in my immediate family had died. And my own health was intact, with my largest health issue an occasional migraine headache. The possibility of disease and death was new to me.

Shortly after the discovery of Graham's problem and after several visits to a surgeon's office, the surgeon persuaded us that the best course of action was an operation. We sat in his office in silence as he described the process of opening the top of Graham's tiny skull to allow him to cut an opening about an inch wide and several inches long. Graham did recover nicely and there were no serious consequences that we were ever aware of, other than flatness on the top of his skull.

After the trauma of surgery, our little family recovered and resumed a life full of wonder and excitement. Every experience with our son was new, a first. We watched with awe as each new skill was developed, each new day brought something we hadn't expected but found incredible. Graham grew and thrived. He was a happy, albeit shy, little guy from the beginning, quick to walk, quick to talk, quick to smile, quick to explore and comprehend the world around him. We watched with the purest kind of joy as the walking became running, the talking became conversations, the smiles became laughter, and the exploration became an insatiable curiosity.

We were proud of our son and so hopeful about his future.

"Oh dear dad can you see me now, I am myself like you somehow, I'll ride the wave where it takes me, now I'll hold the pain. Release me."
– Pearl Jam, *Release*

Chapter 34:
A FATHER'S LOVE

Over the coming years, I would always have a special relationship with my firstborn. His beginning had changed my life forever, and I felt closer to him than almost anyone else. Will, Seth, and Colin changed my life as well. Each brought new joy and concerns. But each birth and each baby and each child was different.

In many ways, the relationship with my oldest son was more intense than it was with my three younger sons. That was better in some ways, and in many ways worse. I was harder on Graham and expected more of him. I was less prepared as a first-time parent and less mature as a person when Graham was so young and impressionable.

With the birth of each of his brothers, I became more relaxed, more experienced, and more capable as a father. A spilled soda in the minivan was a very big deal when Graham was two years old, and much less so when Colin was two. I was tense and yelled at Graham, only to calmly correct Colin when he did the same thing years later.

Despite some rough edges as a father, I did develop a deep, fundamental bond with Graham over the years, unlike anything I've experienced with any other human being. He seemed to pick up on what I cherished in life, such as the outdoors, music, politics, philosophy, and literature. There were few things that Graham found interesting that I did not. We were more than father and son, more than friends; we were kindred souls, as they say.

But even out in nature, when we connected most deeply, I couldn't help but feel sad and inept in the face of Graham's depression—particularly when faced with his nighttime insomnia and his daytime sleep. I witnessed this pattern most acutely on our hiking trips. At least once a year, Graham and I would head out to the Colorado Rockies in the summer or the Arizona desert in the winter. On these backpacking trips, I would awaken early and Graham would sleep late, often for several hours after I had awakened. I would busy myself with camp chores or simply sit and drink coffee. Sometimes I would take off on a morning hike or run. Graham would remain quiet, sleeping deeply in the tent. Though I was near him, watching over him, I felt lonely and sad because his abnormal sleep pattern meant we couldn't share the day. And I knew he'd be certain to awake later with a headache or a deep sense of lethargy and depression. Our trips together accentuated how far Graham's life was from that of someone like myself, who had the luxury of normal cycles of sleep and emotion.

After all those years and all those intense, enjoyable, and sometimes anguished experiences with Graham, I would experience his death as I'd experienced his impending birth: driving, with Mary, on a trip whose destination would change my life forever.

Back in 1981, it was pure excitement and anxious wonder. It was beauty and love in their purest forms.

And it wasn't as if that feeling ever went away. Very few things in this life stay with you until you die, but loving your children is one of them. The clock ticks and almost everything is transient and deciduous, even fleeting. You find something that gives you joy and it seems to slip through your fingers with the passing of time. Great times and great feelings change to worry and doubt. The song stops, the novel closes, and the season comes to an end.

But your love for your child never ends.

On an evening years after Graham's death, Mary and I were getting ready for bed. As always, I was first to pull off my clothes and jump under the covers. Mary walked in from the bathroom a few minutes later, and I looked up from my book as she picked up our cat, Lola, to put her outside our room (Lola has a terrible habit of kneading and scratching on our blanket at the crack of dawn).

But before putting her gently down outside our room, Mary held the cat and stroked her furry head and back. She talked to her in a soft, tender voice, saying she loved her and would see her in the morning. It struck me that I'd seen this before. Mary was holding that cat as if she were a baby, in the crook of her arm, so she could touch her with her other hand. Mary was a mother. Mary was a nurturer.

She had given birth to four beautiful baby boys. Now, with all the boys gone from the home, Mary was still a kind mother. She cared deeply about what was in her hands. She loved.

It made me realize the loving really does not stop. It is enduring. It is forever.

Every morning, Mary gets up, showers, dresses, and dabs a drop of Chanel Mademoiselle perfume on each side of her neck. It is a reminder of Graham, who gave her a bottle of the perfume for Christmas 2004.

Then, walking out of the bathroom, she sometimes pauses to read a brief passage that Graham typed on the computer, printed, and gave to her on Mother's Day, 1998. It's taped to our bedroom wall. It reads:

I love my mother because my mother understands. She cares for me throughout her hardships, as if nothing was going on in her life. She helps me with things I don't yet understand, but most of all, my mother loves me unconditionally. I love you, Mother.

"Beyond the place where time is still, night is day. Across the bridge where angels dwell, children play."
– Van Morrison, *Across the Bridge Where Angels Dwell*

Chapter 35:

DAYS ON MOUNT HERMAN

As I look back, it seems there was a time in our home that was nothing but pure happiness. Of course, time usually does blur memories in a positive way. But the time I remember, the 1980's, was special for our household any way I view it. From 1981 to 1987, we welcomed four baby boys to the world. Mary was pregnant often, and like her body, the atmosphere was expectant and thrilling. And though sometimes the pregnancies and the birthing were far from easy and the subsequent parental chores were exhausting and never-ending, these were good times, very good times.

In the years after Graham died, Seth dug through the boxes of photos from this era and brought them upstairs from the basement to be examined and appreciated. The overriding impression of those photos confirms my own memories of a happy, rambunctious, and a carefree young family. Graham and his younger brothers were alive and vibrant. We were all living out our dreams under the same roof, and I can't help but wonder if Mary and I will ever again achieve that same level of contentment and reward.

We loved all the activity, whether it was the boys riding their plastic cars in our unfinished basement on a Saturday morning, or tucked in their beds to listen to Mary read to them before they fell asleep.

This was a time of baby bottles filled with apple juice, car seats and crumbs in the minivan, and tiny shoes in the hall. The days were more than full, the mornings a rush to get ready for the school bus, the evenings a race to get "tucked in" by Mom and Dad. The boys would run into our closet to pick out their "jammie shirts" for the night from a basket of old T-shirts I had gathered from races, basketball tournaments, and the like. They all had their favorites and looked for them as they reappeared from what seemed to be a constantly churning washing machine. Then the boys would dash toward their bedrooms, their oversized shirts flapping, and finally the energy in the house would be replaced with calm. Those nights and days were a beautiful time in the lives of the six Stingleys.

Graham was the one who took us through a series of family firsts. He was the first to go to preschool when we lived in Lincoln. I remember crying in my car one day as I watched him walk from the car, up the sidewalk, and into the front door of the school. He stopped and turned, held the door open with one hand, and waved good-bye to me, his face a picture of excitement and fear.

Then he was the first to get on a big yellow school bus, Mary walking him down our long, wooded road with his baby brother in her arms. Occasionally I would take Graham to the bus, experiencing the same sad but happy feeling of departure, as he waved to me from the small window of the giant bus.

While writing this book, I accidentally came upon a relic of this fond period of Graham's young life. It was a dog-eared book, *My Book about Me*, signed, "For Graham, I love you, Mommy, Christmas 1985." On the inside front cover was a printed sticker with a picture of a small train carrying a load of books, with the inscription "This Book Belongs to: Graham Stingley." I remembered seeing that sticker on all of Graham's childhood books.

This was a bit of a workbook, one to be filled out by the child in his own handwriting. Most of the blanks were indeed filled in with the details of Graham's young life. He weighed forty-five pounds and was four feet nine inches tall. He wrote that he was "Steven Graham, 265 Lodgepole Way, Monument, CO 80132 and my phone number is 4-88-0265." He added that he lived in a "house in the mountains" and his house had "lots of windows." His favorite food was "chicken, spaghetti, and pizza" but please don't give him "greenbens" and "peas." He checked that he was a "very good student" and had read 100 books, his favorite being *Hop on Pop* by Dr. Seuss. His longest hair was three inches. His favorite sport was "every sport" but he had first written and then scratched out "socor." He said he was "very good" at sports. His favorite song was "Born in the USA"; he did not sing in the bath, but was a great whistler. He said he could make a variety of noises, including a noise like a "football player hiking a ball." When he grew up, he said, he wanted to be a "pro sports player," but had written and then scratched out "private pilot."

At the end of the book were blank pages for writing a story, but they are empty. On the last page there are blanks to fill in the month, day, and year Graham finished writing in the book. They also are blank. As I held the unfinished book in my hands, I cried. I couldn't help seeing the uncompleted book as a metaphor for a life that was not to be completed.

This age of playfulness, innocence, and hope would soon change for Graham and his brothers. There would be complications, conflict, and disappointment. The outside world would influence them through people, places, and situations beyond our or their control. Sometimes the cruel and ugly behavior of the few would sting longer and harder than the beauty of the many. Maybe that is why I liked those days on Lodgepole Way, when the boys seemed protected within the confines of our home. There would be a day when that veil of protection would slowly lift, and the boys would be exposed, not just to the external world, but to their own complex and often confusing internal worlds. Among my memories of those joyful, golden days of our young family, our camping trips on Mount Herman are some of my favorites. These camping excursions took place not far from home, but far from our daily routines. We would load all our camping gear in the back of the Suburban, pack the cooler full of hot dogs, soda pop, and some beer for me, and take off up Mount Herman Road, which wound steeply from Monument into the Front Range mountains.

I remember the anticipation as we bumped along on the rough road. We'd put in a cassette we all liked, maybe Bruce Springsteen, roll down the windows to appreciate the scenery and the cool mountain air, and off we'd go, the dust rolling behind us.

After almost an hour of curling through the mountains and sometimes hugging the sides of canyons, we'd come upon our usual campsite. It seemed to provide us with all that we needed: a relatively flat piece of land for our tent and a perfect perch for our campfire at the top of a huge rock. From that perch, we had an absolutely magnificent view of Pikes Peak nearly twenty miles to the southwest. The land dropped away steeply, so our rock was ground level on one end and twenty feet high on the other, giving us a nice "on top of the world" feeling. Surrounding us was a dense and healthy forest that stretched in every direction for miles, and afforded ample opportunity for exploring.

This was our special campsite. This was our perfect mountain retreat.

The boys loved it. They were free to roam, either on foot or on the bikes that we would haul precariously on the back of the Suburban. The bikes were cheap entertainment for us all. We would ride down Mount Herman Road, which had little traffic, or explore small Jeep trails that often led nowhere.

We roasted hot dogs on sticks, then sandwiched burnt marshmallows and chocolate between graham crackers to make the very popular s'mores. The boys constantly stirred and poked at the campfire with anything they could find: sticks, shoes, and the like. I will never forget our boys' early and long-lasting fascination with all of the basic elements of nature, particularly fire and water. The imperatives of those caveman genes were enough to occupy and entertain them for hours.

Of course, we also brought along our constant companions, Sally, the basset hound, and Scooter, the golden retriever. One time Sally wandered off and could not be found for an hour or so. There was much drama and commotion, and our little search party looked high and low, up the ridge and down into the ravines. Finally, as the panic reached a crescendo, she trotted toward us, instantly restoring the happiness and well-being that I still associate with these outings.

For the trip home, we'd load everything up but the bikes, and I would slowly drive down the mountain, keeping a careful watch in my rearview mirror on the elated (and dusty) group of four brothers riding their bikes down the mountain road behind me, enjoying gravity and screaming their elation.

Seth told me as I was writing this book that was the first time he could remember having "absolute fun," when he rode with his three brothers down Mount Herman Road. From my perspective watching the scene from the comfort of my driver's seat, I couldn't have agreed with him more.

"So I walk up on high and I step to the edge to see the world below."
– Collective Soul, *The World I Know*

Chapter 36:

RUNNING DOWN THE MOUNTAIN

As I have done so many times over the years, I recently hiked to the summit of Mount Herman, that broad, sloping sentinel over Monument. On the way down, I had the urge to run. Encouraged by the pull of the earth's gravity, I began to jog and pick up speed over the rocky trail.

As often happens when I'm running in the mountains, a vivid memory came to the forefront of my mind from somewhere deep inside. I remembered the very first time I climbed Mount Herman. I went with a friend visiting from Nebraska, and we took Graham and my friend's son of the same age, Karl, who is not the same Karl that became Graham's friend later. Judging from a photograph I came across years later, Graham was about six years old. He was dressed in sweat pants, a T-shirt, and a small, red cap. With his buddy in the photo, he was holding up his arms on the summit to show his muscles, a tiny mountaineer.

It was one of those perfect Colorado mornings when we tackled the nine-thousand-foot mountain. Getting up there was no small feat, especially for the two with small feet. But when we arrived at the summit (which I would learn later was not the real summit) we all relished in our accomplishment. The boys celebrated first and then excitedly ran around to every rocky perch that looked down upon the plains to the east and the miles of rolling mountains to the west. Since then, I've been on mountain tops, big and small, all over the world, and never have I felt as proud as that day.

On our descent, we walked slowly and carefully down the first steep, especially rocky stretch, but then the trail became smoother and flatter. That is the point at which I remember our young boys suddenly breaking into a run. Led by Graham, the boys succumbed to the thrilling pull of the earth's power.

I don't remember being especially alarmed, but my friend from the flatlands panicked. He yelled at them to stop running, and quickly caught up with Karl to chastise and warn him. I think I may have joined meekly in my friend's warnings, but I distinctly remember feeling he was being too cautious and overcorrecting, and that running down the trail was not only okay for these youngsters, but their reward for working so hard and climbing up the mountain in the first place.

I also remember Graham and Karl continuing to run from time to time, always to the chagrin and loud warnings of my friend, and to my silent amusement.

So, there I was, some twenty years later, running down the same mountain and loving it. I was thrilled with the wind in my face and gravity's force on my weight. I was careful. I've always been cautious in the mountains, especially when alone. I didn't want my nearly two-hundred-pound body to be flung headfirst down the rocky trail, as has been the case in a few of my mountain runs. But I was enjoying the experience. It made me feel like a six-year-old.

And as I ran, I envisioned my young son running down the mountain, with the screeches of my overwrought friend fading in the background, but with the quiet approval of his father letting him go, letting him experience life at full speed. How good it must have felt.

I fretted briefly over whether my permissive style might have worked to Graham's disadvantage later in his life. Did I not impose enough control, discipline, warnings? Or by allowing him to run when he wanted, to take risks in his life, did I encourage him to embrace exploration, freedom, and happiness? As my firstborn, Graham bore the brunt of my fledgling ways of fatherhood, with my own imperfect skills and philosophies, my own youthful mistakes and sometimes misguided passions.

I'll never really know how my particular brand of fathering affected my son's life—or death. I'll continue to mull the questions, but I'm not sure the answers will be revealed to me. I do know that on that beautiful Colorado day, Graham enjoyed running down that mountain.

He kept running in his life, loving the thrill of speed, through one grand and often scary experience after another. He was a man of the moment, running, often without regard for his own safety, taking in the rush of time through his mind and his body, perhaps his soul.

As the years went by and those six-year-old days vanished, I watched Graham run, often unrestrained, with the wind blowing in his face, his blond hair flying, and gravity pulling him earthward.

"Saw a shooting star tonight, and I thought of you. You were tryin' to break into another world, a world I never knew. I always kind of wondered, if you ever made it through."

– Bob Dylan, *Shooting Star*

Chapter 37:
A YOUNG STAR

Graham lived a fuller life than most young men could have imagined. He was not one to take the careful or easy route. He seemed to choose the more challenging and often riskier, if perhaps more rewarding, path at every turn of his young life.

Perhaps it was his intelligence that drove him. From an early age, Graham exhibited an ability to quickly assimilate, retain, and build upon what he had learned. He was early to talk, and his language skills throughout his life were superb. Teachers in his elementary school would tell us how bright he was, and he was in accelerated classes by the end of elementary school.

In middle school, as he became more disenchanted with the education system and culture he saw each day at school and after, Graham started learning on his own. He read a lot from an early age. And though the Internet was difficult to access when he was younger, he seemed to master whatever technology that was necessary to get information on the subjects that interested him, including music, religion, science, literature, and philosophy. At some point in his early life, he transitioned from a school-taught child to a self-taught young man.

The friends he sought were by and large inquisitive people, as well. They talked about how the world was and how it should be, their burgeoning knowledge and youthful idealism growing together. In the midst of this flourishing intellectualism, I saw Graham and a few of his closest friends adopt more radical and extreme ideas, as their disappointment with their own state of affairs and their alienation from the conventional world accelerated. Perhaps their explorations of the socialism of Karl Marx, the atheism of Frederick Nietzsche, and the like were merely intellectual games for clever—and bored—young men. But I saw them pursue these unconventional lines of thought and behavior with a passion that bordered on zeal, sometimes raising the eyebrows of their parents, their teachers, and their peers.

There also was the very powerful influence of music. I saw Graham's taste in music shift from youthful, happy songs, to much more serious artists and on to the darker genres of death and black metal. He went from They Must be Giants to Pink Floyd to Burning Witch. Of course it was a gradual progression, as Graham tasted many kinds of music along the way, from classical to blues to punk. But whatever musical phase Graham was exploring at the time, he took music very seriously, and I know he was greatly affected by what he listened to.

Graham was also part of an ongoing and ever-changing group of people who spent a great deal of time trying to create and play their own music. Although I don't think he ever achieved great skill on the guitar, which was his chosen instrument. Graham started his musical pursuit first with piano lessons, then onto acoustic guitar lessons. I saw him gradually progress on a used piano we muscled into the living room, then onto various, cheap guitars until, as a Christmas present, we gave him a Les Paul guitar that was his most prized possession. His family still quietly covets that guitar, although it sits quiet and encased in the storage room of our home, perhaps too powerful of a memory to see the light of day.

I do remember a time when Graham, his good friend Karl, and a couple other close friends made an appearance at Karl's school, Palmer High School, in downtown Colorado Springs, at the student musical show. When they got on stage, Graham and Karl's band completely shifted the mood of that variety show. The stage was barely lit, and the four young men played dark and foreboding backup on their guitars while Karl moaned and growled at the microphone. It was quite the intense scene and I loved it, sitting among mostly high school students and a few parents. After years of listening to and loving music, Graham finally got *his* night on the stage. I was so proud and happy for him. At least for that one night he was a star.

It seemed an appropriate anecdote to the story of his life so far, one of a life without public applause. Particularly painful, I think, was being rejected from middle-school and then high-school freshman basketball teams. It wasn't until he was a sophomore in high school that he made the team, only to sit on the bench in humiliation most of the season. His attempt to play football was similarly frustrating for him. They didn't cut kids in seventh-grade football, so Graham made the team. But again, he didn't get to play and suffered the agony of standing, dressed and ready, on the sidelines, watching his peers have fun.

For all his perceived failures in the sports arena, Graham didn't give up. He especially loved basketball and tried out for three years before finally making the team as a sophomore. I was at my parents' house in Lincoln when he called me and told me he had made the team. I had not heard such excitement and pride in his voice. But the season did not play out well for Graham. He sat on the bench while others got to play. On the rare occasion he was called into play, he was so nervous he didn't do well. I recently saw a picture of him on the court dressed in his Number 11 uniform—was it coincidence that 11 has always been my favorite number? He had a nervous smile on his face. It would be the last athletic photo of Graham for that yearbook or any after that.

Graham's athletic rejections might have pained him all the more because his younger brothers had exceptional success from an early age. Will had an uncanny talent for basketball and ended up being an all-state star on an exceptional team. Seth was tall, lean, and very good at basketball as well, starring on his teams from an early age. Colin was good at basketball but excelled in high school football as a wide receiver. He broke the records for number of yards by a receiver for the season with his often-spectacular catches and long touchdown runs.

This all played out against a backdrop of our family's overall love of sports. Not only did high school athletics consume our lives during those days, but we also had Denver Nuggets and Broncos season tickets and went often as a family to those events. And though I personally wasn't as much of a sports fan as the rest of the family, I was grateful to be able to play basketball well enough in high school to garner the attention of the homecoming queen, at a time when I was painfully shy and would have disappeared into the background.

For his brothers' games, Graham was often in the stands cheering on his brothers. But as his father, I couldn't help but be sad when I looked down the bleacher and saw my son impassioned by the game he was watching, screaming with joy when his brothers scored or yelling at the referee when he made a call against their teams. This was my oldest son who would never have the opportunity to be on that court or that field, having his brothers cheer for him. And when the game was over, and the attention focused on the stars, Graham would avoid the fuss about his brothers, because it had to be just too much. I didn't blame him. I can still see him in my mind, walking slowly out of the gym's exit into the night.

"Resting in the fields, far from the turbulent space, half asleep near the stars with a small dog licking your face. Jokerman dance to the nightingale tune, bird fly high by the light of the moon. Ohh, ohh, jokerman."

– Bob Dylan, *Jokerman*

Chapter 38:

JOKERMAN

I recognized my own youthful traits in Graham. I had always wanted to be different, and at times was driven to resist conformity and seek my own unique identity. It seemed I had passed the rebel gene onto my son. But he, like all my sons in their own ways, exceeded my ability and need to question the accepted order of things. They were better at understanding the world around them than I would ever be; they were simply better educated and better informed. It was as if my own offspring continued a microevolution in our family's history. But this evolution appeared to be occurring rapidly, so rapidly I imagined my grandparents really wouldn't recognize my sons' traits as their own. I suppose part of this microevolution was also due to my marriage to Mary, that homecoming queen I have referred to and the daughter of a prominent and well-respected family in our small Kansas town. More refined and worldly than I, Mary brought to our relationship and eventually our family a maturity and stability that our boys and I wouldn't have otherwise been exposed to. Together with my wildness and her civility, we passed on a combination of traits, values, and behavior that differed substantially from both her family and mine.

The cultures I grew up in—both inside and outside the home—did in fact stress temperance, tradition, caution, and convention. Pushing limits of any kind was not encouraged—in fact, it was discouraged. Questioning authority or cultural institutions was also frowned upon. Maybe my family simply reflected its small-town, rural, middle-America environment. This culture was by no means all bad. To this day, when I revisit my homeland, I am immediately reminded of the kind, loyal, and loving nature of the people living there.

The culture in which I was raised cannot be understood without the context of religion, and specifically the strong Protestant influence that hung over the land like the frequent damp fogs on Sunday mornings. In my own youth, spurred on by the cultural revolution going on around me, I began to question the widely held beliefs and customs of society as I had grown to know and accept them. I was an observer, not a participant, in the hippie subculture and political activism of the 1960s; I remember telling a friend in college that I felt as if we were living in the aftermath of something big, something more significant than I could fully understand. All the activism of that period was surely affecting our lives, even though we had not been a direct part of its creation.

Like mine, Graham's early childhood environment outside the home was conservative, reflecting the ubiquitous military and evangelical Christian presence in Colorado Springs. El Paso County was the home of not one but several Air Force installations, including the prestigious U.S. Air Force Academy located literally across the road from Monument, plus a very large army post that sprawls for miles on the outskirts of the city. Many retired military families either stayed in or returned to Monument after being stationed in Colorado Springs.

The other large group of people who inhabited our little world was evangelical Christian. Colorado Springs houses the headquarters of more than a hundred such organizations, ranging from worldwide missionary groups to youth groups to publishers of church materials and books.

It was no wonder outsiders considered Colorado a stronghold for the conservative, the religious, and the Republican Party.

Graham's schools educated more than their fair share of the offspring of driven, fervent followers of Jesus Christ. And unlike the quiet, polite churchgoing people I had grown up with, these people were not as shy about proclaiming their religious beliefs.

Graham's environment seemed to philosophically push him in the opposite direction—in part because our immediate family was neither military nor Christian, and Mary and I as parents had fostered a liberal and open-minded point of view in the home. Though we always encouraged a general acceptance of all beliefs and opinions, I think the general tone of our home predisposed the boys to be at least skeptical of exclusive attitudes. This was especially true of Graham, because at an early age he became very interested in and well-informed about religion, government, and philosophy. I remember being amazed at how much he knew about the world, both from a historical and current perspective. He would watch the news, read books, and listen to his teachers, and then make sense of it all. He was a quick study. I remember learning that Graham, at a fairly young age, was receiving e-mail from an American atheist organization. I also spotted books like the *Communist Manifesto* and *Thus Spoke Zarathustra* lying around his room. This both alarmed me a bit and impressed me. Most boys his age were more interested in sports and girls than the nature of the universe and whether there was a God or not, or what economic system was the best. This was a young man who was obviously very hungry for knowledge and for answers to life's bigger questions.

It was interesting to see him rebel against capitalism and Christianity, because for all our liberalism, our own family was clearly supported by capitalism and held many Christian values (although both, in their rawest forms, made us uncomfortable). Mary's family owned community banks in three states, a small business empire built by the hard work and entrepreneurial drive of her father over many years. And though her father's drive and perpetual absence from family life caused other issues within my wife's family, it created a not-so-small amount of wealth that allowed for financial security and material well being for everyone in the family.

But Graham's intellectual explorations were more of a game than a heartfelt cause. He never rejected us because of our family's economic or religious foundations. He loved taking contrarian views on almost anything, from economics and music to shoe styles. This contrarian disposition made school frustrating for him, since the system seemed to play to the average intelligence and the comfort of popular culture. The contrast between his conservative childhood peers and his liberal household also seemed to cause conflict and health problems for him. I saw him turn increasingly to his own methods of learning, through books, movies, and people outside mainstream America.

In fact, it seemed Graham was bent on rejection of the normal and acceptance of the abnormal. This made it difficult for him to find acceptance from his peers or those in authority. He mistrusted many of them, and some mistrusted him. And where there is no trust, there is no respect. I saw Graham become increasingly angry and hostile toward his peers and authority figures as he went through high school. It wasn't until well after high school that his staunchly held beliefs and views began to mellow, and he became more accepting of the world around him.

"What is lost, what is missing? What's been gone way to long? We had dreams when the night was young. We were believers when the night was young."
– Robbie Robertson, *When the Night was Young*

Chapter 39:

MARLON BRANDO OF MOTOWN

Despite his physical afflictions and frequent bouts of depression and anxiety, Graham mustered the energy and courage to attempt something of a normal life; even so much as what might be called an active social life. One of his special passions was music, and he pursued it both as a participant and a fan with all the fervor he could muster. Music seemed to be the primary bond among his closest friends, who regularly went to concerts of bands of both local and national renown. The names of the local bands I don't recall, although I remember sometimes being puzzled if not somewhat alarmed at their monikers. The nationally known bands included the likes of Sepultura, Metallica, Primus, Black Sabbath and Pantera. A few times Graham was kind enough to let me go with him to a concert that wasn't one of my choosing, say Bob Dylan or Neil Young. I remember vividly one our firsts, a festival at Red Rocks that featured Live and Offspring. Later, there was a particularly memorable—if not slightly frightening—concert at Mile High Stadium that included Marilyn Manson and was headlined by Ozzy Osborne.

But as Graham grew older we went to concerts less often and his mainstay was going with his friends, as well it should have been.

For a couple of years, he and several of his friends hung out at a record store in central Colorado Springs called the Mosh Pit. There, they sat, smoked cigarettes, listened for hours to music, and talked. In late high school and after, he spent hours and sometimes days away from home with these friends. They would create and play music, go to concerts in small venues along the Front Range, and generally enjoy themselves, as far as I could tell. Needless to say, I'm sure there was a fair amount of alcohol and marijuana available to smooth the ride. Graham was at first a hold-out from dope smoking, a friend of his told me, but eventually began the practice in earnest in the fall of 1999. He would continue the habit for the rest of his life, reminding me from time to time that it was the only thing that really kept his depression at bay.

Friends recalled to me later that Graham was a leader of the pack, albeit a quiet one. He had an easy way, but was clever and funny in a way that his peers enjoyed.

"He was the Marlon Brando of Motown," his friend Karl told me once, using their nickname for Monument. "He was the Steve McQueen of Monument. Even the kids who weren't as intellectual as Graham looked up to and respected Graham as the cool guy. He was at the epicenter of the disenfranchised youth of his area, where it was okay to be a 'fuck-up' and a radical thinker, where it was okay to just enjoy people who enjoyed the same weird things as you did, the metal music and the dark, subversive attitude it fostered."

Perhaps because of his own internal emotional battles, or perhaps because of his own supercharged sensitivity, Graham was empathic about the suffering of others. Graham earned Karl's respect early on in their friendship by seeming to understand Karl's sadness and confusion over the sudden death of his father. "He really understood, and that meant a lot to me. He understood me as well as anyone ever had. Honestly, today, if I could have my dad back or Graham back, I'd take Graham back."

During this period, Graham kept reading, spurred by Karl's own literary interests. His range widened and deepened to include Camus, Tolstoy, Hemingway, Hunter S. Thompson, Vonnegut, Nietzsche, and Steinbeck. Herman Hesse, a favorite of my own in my youth, became one of his favorites. He related strongly to the character in *Beneath the Wheel*, and later to the troubled protagonist in *Steppenwolf*.

His reading continued right up to the end. One day, looking through some of the stuff from his apartment, I found a couple of plastic bags full of books he had purchased in 2004. My eyes filled with tears as I pulled the unread books from each shopping bag. One by one, I slowly examined them, reading the back cover if I wasn't familiar with the book.

The first book I held with my trembling hands was *The Call of Cthulhu and Other Weird Stories* by H. P. Lovecraft, who, according to the back-cover praise by Stephen King, "has yet to be surpassed as the twentieth century's greatest practitioner of the classic horror tale."

Next was *Songs of Innocence and of Experience* by William Blake, whom the back cover calls "an independent and rebellious thinker, who abhorred pretension and falsity in others. His Songs of Innocence are products of this innocent imagination untainted by worldliness, while the Songs of Experience resulted from his feelings of indignation and pity for the sufferings of mankind."

There were also the five-hundred-page novel *The Last Temptation of Christ* by Nikos Kazantzakis and *The Genealogy of Morals and Ecce Homo* by Friedrich Nietzsche, an author I have failed to understand but who was one of Graham's early favorites. There were *Chronicles, Volume One* and *Tarantula*, both by Bob Dylan; *Farewell to Arms* and *Men without Women* by Ernest Hemingway; *The Fox, the Captain's Doll, the Ladybird* by D. H. Lawrence; *The Mysterious Stranger and Other Stories* by Mark Twain; *Cannery Row* by John Steinbeck; *Breakfast of Champions* by Kurt Vonnegut; *In Our Time* and *Candide*; and the *Tao Te Ching* by Lao Tzu.

Finally, there was a small paperback book with a bookmark halfway through, a Broncos ticket stub for the game against the Carolina Panthers from October 10, 2004. The book is *Notes from Underground* by Fyodor Dostoevsky. The introduction by Donald Fanger read:

> *I am a sick man...I am a spiteful man,"* the irascible voice of a nameless narrator cries out. And so, from underground, emerge the passionate confessions of a suffering man; the brutal self-examination of a tormented soul; the bristling scorn and iconoclasm of an alienated individual who has become one of the greatest antiheroes in all literature.

And finally, as a non-literary exclamation point to his taste in art, I found a small color poster of Vincent van Gogh's "Skull of a Skeleton with Burning Cigarette," an apt title for what was painted.

The list of books provided an accurate snapshot of Graham's literary life. It also shows that his artistic tastes and his views of the world were diverse and evolving; that his ideas were becoming more refined, as he found what really worked and what was really true.

His radical high school years and later mellowing were also the natural maturation that any young person goes through. As some of the emotional wounds from his disastrous middle-school era began to heal, Graham became more comfortable with his true self, and his need to be extreme or be different lessened.

But those middle-school years truly had been excruciating. A face full of acne, repeated, failed tryouts for the school sports teams, and an inability to converse, let alone cuddle, with girls were just too much for this sister-less, sensitive young man to handle. "Let me tell you one thing," Karl said to me once. "The people we were hanging out with, the music we were listening to, and the concerts we were going to weren't exactly conducive to meeting girls or even thinking about girls in a healthy way."

It may have been the way he and his friends were behaving, but I know Graham really wanted it differently. "There are times I want a girlfriend so bad it hurts," Graham told me once. "I just don't know how to go about it."

"Old man, look at my life, I'm a lot like you. I need someone to love me the whole day through. Ah, one look in my eyes and you can tell that's true."
— Crosby, Stills, Nash and Young, *Old Man Take a Look at My Life*

Chapter 40:

HEADACHES AND HEARTACHES

One day, in a year I can't pinpoint in my memory, Graham was sprawled in a chair in the corner of the kitchen/dining room of our home, a chair where he often slept soundly as the normal commotion of the household continued around him. This day, this moment, he was not asleep, but seemed defeated, tired. As I walked by, he looked up and said to me, "I feel like all I've done in the past five years of my life is gain twenty pounds."

I remember so vividly that he then told me he felt like an "old man" and pronounced with some certainty to me that "I'm going to die before you do, Pops."

He indeed had gained weight since high school, when he was a slim, tall, and active kid. Weight gain was one of the first side effects listed for the headache medicines he took, and he was suffering from it. It was one more strike of misfortune in a world that seemed to go against Graham. Not that his habits were healthy—he ate at Taco Bell often and only tried to exercise occasionally, coming back from a brief run with sweat pouring down his red face. Graham also smoked cigarettes, a habit he picked up early and continued for the rest of his short life.

I worried about his nutrition, his fitness, and his general well-being every day, but in retrospect I did little to help him change. I worried more about his depression and his alienation from himself and the world. Better nutrition and fitness could come later in life, I thought, when he moved beyond the thick morass of youth and depression. I just knew that he would get beyond these demons that plagued him, and lead a healthy, productive, and fulfilling life. I just knew that in my heart, although I ached nonetheless for him every day.

His doctors also noted his unhealthy habits. At one point, Mary and I pushed our local family-practice physician to give a written recommendation so Graham could undergo testing and hopefully treatment at the Mayo Clinic in Minnesota. As his health problems continued to mount and intensify, his treatment by various specialist physicians in Colorado Springs and Denver seemed inadequate. No one seemed to either care about or be able to cure the whole Graham.

But the meeting with the doctor didn't go well. The doctor seemed more preoccupied with Graham's lack of good habits than what might be *causing* his lack of good habits. He didn't seem to be able to look deep enough to even allow Graham to be examined by doctors at Mayo or somewhere else who would and could look deep enough. Graham should quit smoking, eat less, and start running; this pompous and ignorant doctor lectured Graham. That would begin to solve all his problems.

In the end, after several long weeks of waiting, the doctor called and said his request to admit Graham to the Mayo Clinic had been denied. I was angry and disappointed, but not surprised. It may have been an opportunity of a lifetime for Graham—an opportunity missed, and perhaps fatal.

Every time Graham's depression loosened its grip, his recovery would seem to be derailed by severe, long-lasting headaches. These headaches would keep him in bed for hours and seemingly days. There he lay, in his darkened bedroom, day and night, with debilitating headaches.

We took Graham to a headache specialist first in Denver, then in Chicago. The recommendation was always the same. They would suggest changing the medication prescribed previously either by them or some other doctor. Then, when that recommendation didn't seem to help they would make yet another adjustment, often to a drug more powerful with more powerful side effects. These changes also typically involved tapering down the dosage of one drug over time before ramping up on another. So there were these in between adjustment periods that were hard on Graham. It seemed he was caught in an endless loop of ineffective medication.

A report from the Denver neurological doctor Graham saw only a few times in 2004 gives a clear snapshot of what he had been going through for years. The report starts out with a summary very familiar to Graham, Mary and myself, and then ends with a surprising new treatment technique that Graham readily accepted, but as far as I could tell it would end up being yet another failed attempt to help.

The report read:

Date: 09-29-2004

Name: Stingley, S. Graham

Problem: Migraine with aura. Neck pain. History of psychiatric disorder.

The patient was last seen in the office 07-06-2004.

History: The patient's mother called on 9-10-04 to report that the patient was vomiting and having migraines almost daily. At that time he was taking Zomig for his headaches; he was sleeping almost all day. I returned the call and suggested decreasing Topamax from 100mg/day to 75mg/day and to call to report on the effect of the change. His mother called again on 9-13-04 to report that the patient was still taking the Topamax 25mg two tablets twice a day (100mg/day). He had not started the Parnate but planned to do so later that week. Reduction of the Topamax to 25mg AM and continuing at the two 25mg tabs in PM was suggested; he was to keep the appointment for today, 9-29-04.

The patient says he is still having problems with headaches, nausea, and vomiting. He is taking Zomig 2.5mg for headaches which seem to come four to five times a week. He says headaches last "quite a while, 8-9 hours at least." Headaches are maximal left sub occipital area. Note: he denies head/back injuries.) He is not aware of headache triggers. Headaches are worse now than several months ago.

Medications by history:

Topamax 15mg, one AM and two PM
Zomig 2.5mg one at the onset of migraine
Lexapro 20mg one a day
Navane 2.5mg one a day
Clonazepam 0.5mg two at night; one in AM
Tylenol at the onset of headache

Neurological examination:

Patient is alert, fluent, and cooperative. He drove here from Colorado Springs.

BP 124/88, sitting pulse 86, weight 217#

Then in the report there is detail of the doctor's neurological exam which indicates there are no obvious neurological problems to be detected, other than some "very tender" spots in Graham's head and neck. The doctor's assessment then states the obvious.

"His headaches and nausea are worrisome," he concludes. "Due to the chronicity and the refractory nature of his headaches, coupled with the fairly prominent tenderness of upper cervical muscles, is such that I recommend a trial of BOTOX for his headaches. I have discussed the use of BOTOX with the patient and he is very interested in proceeding with the injections today (he lives in Colorado Springs.)"

Of course Graham was "very interested." He felt terrible all the time and wanted to feel better. He had been to so many doctors who had prescribed so many things and nothing seemed to work. BOTOX surprised me because I thought it was for older women, who want to look younger, not a young man who wanted not to feel like a sick old man.

"The woods are lovely, dark and deep. But I have promises to keep, and miles to go before I sleep."

– Robert Frost, *Miles to Go*

Chapter 41:

FINAL DAYS

Graham's friends said they saw him changing in the year before his death, becoming closer to his family and more comfortable with himself. And there was evidence that Graham was beginning to see girls, sometimes romantically.

"His family was becoming even more important to him," Karl Deiotte, Graham's long-time friend, told me. "It had always been important to him but it was getting even more so. He loved hanging out with his brothers and would talk about them all the time. He wanted that more and more."

Karl said Graham loved our frequent family trips and camping excursions. "Those things were good for Graham. He'd always wanted to be so independent, but he was changing. He loved those trips and times with the family. He really had this feeling for family."

Because of the age difference—Graham was three years older than Will, four years older than Seth, and six years older than Colin—the boys had been in separate worlds growing up. Also, his younger brothers were so involved year-round in their sports that they saw little of each other. But as the three oldest boys were all living in Denver in the month before Graham's death, they were spending increasing amounts of time together.

Graham also enjoyed spending time in his apartment's mezzanine-floor lounge bar. The forty-some-story apartment building housed an Embassy Suites Hotel on the lower floors. The bar was typical of a hotel's, with dark lighting, constantly blaring TVs, and businessmen and other hotel patrons stopping by for a quick drink or dinner. Karl said Graham would frequently go down to the bar at night, usually dressed in his sweats and slippers for something to drink and eat.

"There he was, hanging out at this lounge with all the businessmen in suits, drinking a Coke and having a snack," Karl said, chuckling. "He loved going down there."

Karl said Graham struck up a relationship with one of the night bartenders. They often would talk and, he thinks, even go back to Graham's room from time to time. Her name was Mary. "They really liked each other," Karl told me. "I think that may have been more than a casual relationship."

Graham had never mentioned this new friend, Mary, to me, but when Karl told me this story in the weeks after Graham died, I tracked her down by phone and had a fifteen-minute conversation. She said she hadn't learned yet what had happened to Graham, but noticed he hadn't been around lately. When I first told her, there was silence on the phone. I think she was crying. She told me what a wonderful person Graham was and how she had enjoyed getting to know him in the brief time they had. She agreed to meet me for coffee or lunch and said she would call me back. I didn't hear from her and tried to call a couple of times but got no message. Finally, a few weeks later, when I called I got a recorded message that the number had been discontinued and was no longer in service. At that point I quit trying to reach her, because I decided if she really wanted to meet me to talk about Graham she would have called me.

One morning in early February, I met Graham for breakfast in the Embassy Suites restaurant. As always, I enjoyed his company, and we chatted openly (I can't remember the topics except that they were engaging as usual). He seemed tired and was sloppily dressed and ungroomed. I worried that he seemed slightly incoherent and slow, probably because he hadn't slept well the night before or perhaps because of his medications. Mornings were never good for Graham.

After breakfast, I walked over to a post office across the street. I needed to renew my passport, so I filled out the forms and had my picture taken. I look happy in the picture, but older with my graying beard and receding hairline. The new passport was sent to me after Graham died. When I opened it, one of the first things I noticed was the official date of issue: February 18, 2005.

Every time I get that passport out and open it to the front page, with the date of issue glaring cold at me, I want to cry.

"Two things fill the mind with ever new and increasing admiration and reverence, the more often and the more steadily one reflects on them: the starry heavens above me and the moral law within me."

– Immanuel Kant

Chapter 42:

INTO THE WILDERNESS

I opened my eyes to a faint, gray light illuminating the thin nylon fabric that separated me from the outside world. Was it moonlight or the dawn? As my senses awakened, I had my answer. Night was over and morning was here. It was time once again to get out of my warm sleeping bag, squeeze my aching body out of the tiny tent, and breathe the cold morning air.

Another day in the wilderness had begun.

The hardest part of spending eighteen days in the mountains was getting up in the morning. My shoulders and hips always hurt from the restless night spent on a pad less than an inch thick. Though I stayed warm in my goose-down bag, it was often below forty degrees in the morning. To extend the discomfort, the high peaks to the east kept my campsite in shadow until late morning.

Why would I choose to spend so many nights in what can be such a hostile environment, with little to shelter me from the cold, rain, and wind? The question only bothered me in early predawn, when I woke to the thin air at eleven thousand feet. This was the time of day when the feelings of loneliness and despair were the strongest. Then the sunlight would eventually hit my camp and warm everything in its glow, myself included. My spirits would change, and the day would brighten.

Like every day, this morning I started my tiny stove, made coffee, and studied my surroundings as I sipped. All around me mountains rose severely from the valley floor. My gaze traced the path of a tumbling, snowmelt stream. As I glanced higher, the water cascaded over a cliff before giving way to snow fields and huge, rocky walls several thousand feet above where I sat. I imagined climbing to these places, as I had so often when I was younger. Now such a climb seemed less likely and too arduous, dangerous. Now I simply enjoyed daydreaming my way around the lofty and impossible places I saw in every direction, ensconced in my sunny perch on the valley floor.

I sat with my coffee for some time, like a lazy backcountry tourist. Only a hundred feet below me, an ice-cold stream noisily raced over rocks, through grassy slopes, and toward the larger valley below. From time to time, I spotted a brook trout swimming in the stream's calm pools. The constant sound of the water moving over the rocks was always reassuring to me, especially when I lay awake in my tent at night listening to the unseen, wild world outside.

One of the attractions of backpacking for me is that I can go about the day with everything I need on my shoulders. This gives me at least a temporary feeling of successfully limiting my possessions to the essentials, a freedom from the things that normally occupy my life. Here, I had to survive and be happy with what I had, a feeling that was harder to realize at home. Today I would walk more than five miles up and over a high mountain saddle, then down into an adjacent wilderness valley before making camp. It was nearly midmorning when I began my arduous day's hike up the trail.

I had chosen this unfamiliar hike in order to mimic my eldest son's eighteen-day Outward Bound trip some twelve years earlier. This is an area of staggering alpine beauty, the high-reaching backbone of the Elk Mountains contrasting with deep, wet valleys. Wildflowers were everywhere, of every color and species. Small and large streams seemed to flow down each little crevice. Seemingly absent were the deadly beetles and perennial droughts that were plaguing much of the Rocky Mountains; the forests and meadows were lush, green, and vibrant.

But it wasn't beauty that brought me here, I reflected as I walked slowly up the next incline with my heavy pack. Rather, it was to discover something about my son's death that would make some sense. One friend suggested I wanted to "be" with Graham. Another friend offered that I was looking for "inner peace." Yet another speculated it was myself that I was trying to find, to reconnect with. *To know the world is beautiful; to know yourself is wisdom*, I kept thinking to myself as I walked along, paraphrasing the tenet of the Tao Te Ching, which I was rereading on my trip.

I'm not sure any of that made sense to me. There was nothing about any of this that made sense to me, and I thought that I would just have to walk until something did. So I walked, sweating in the afternoon sun, my pack creaking rhythmically on my back. I walked through park-like meadows and deep forests. Everywhere I went, I was greeted by a pristine beauty that made me smile, and a deep silence that made me sad. I saw few people, and my chance encounters with humans along the trail were brief, cryptic, and meaningless to me.

On several occasions, I did have visitors who meant something to me. My son Will and his girlfriend Tara joined me for a couple of nights, as did my son Seth later in the trip. My brother-in-law Adam and his climbing partner, Scott, spent a night with me before they climbed one of Colorado's toughest fourteen-thousand-foot mountains. My friend Donovan met me on the trail and spent some time with me as well. My times with these friends and family perfectly counterbalanced my time alone. Companionship was more pleasant and enjoyable than solitude, but it was by being alone that I could find my most powerful reflections. Both were satisfying and rewarding for me; they just allowed for different mindsets and provided me different meaning.

The nice thing about backpacking was the endless hours spent on the trail, generally by yourself even when with a group. Because of the nature of backcountry trails, hikers had to walk single file down narrow trails, making it hard to carry on conversations. In other words, under most circumstances, a hiker finds himself alone with his thoughts.

And of course the thinking ranged from the silly and absurd, to the complex and meaningful. As I walked during this particular trip, my grief hung heavy on my mind, just as my pack hung heavy on my back. Many of my thoughts were troubling or worrisome. Why did my son die? Where is he now? What is this thing I'm experiencing, being a breathing body walking on this round planet spinning in such a large space? What kind of person am I? What kind of father have I been? And so my mind rolled on in an endless stream of questions, questions of the largest and most significant level.

By late afternoon on this particular day of my trip, I began to search the landscape ahead for a spot to camp. It would be good to be near water so I could easily filter my drinking supply and clean myself. I also looked for trees so I could use the dead branches on the ground to fuel an evening fire. It was often hard to find a spot for my tiny tent in this land of steep slopes. When I finally found a campsite with all these elements, it was a pleasant relief, like a silent welcome home. I eagerly set about pitching my tent for another night, pumping and filtering water from the stream, organizing my pack, and collecting firewood. I enjoyed the many chores involved in meeting my basic needs. Even simple things that were easy at home became pleasantly tedious and time-consuming endeavors.

That kind of welcome mindlessness also surfaced when I came face-to-face with the spectacular in this often-spectacular wilderness. For example, a few days before, I had climbed to an alpine lake at the base of fourteen-thousand-foot Capital Peak, one of the most strikingly beautiful mountains I'd seen in Colorado—or indeed anywhere. From there I hiked my way around the ice-cold, dark, blue-green lake, up to a pass that exceeded eleven thousand feet. As I sat on the pass, I studied my map for somewhere to explore next and quickly spotted an unnamed peak to the north, just up the pass on a broad, grassy, rocky ridge. The peak elevation was marked at twelve thousand, seven hundred fifty-one feet, the highest point I would climb on my entire trip.

After about an hour of steady climbing, I reached the summit. A note pad and pen had been left in a clean Starbucks coffee bottle, so I marked the date and wrote the words "In memory of Graham." Silently, then out loud, I named the peak "Graham Mountain." I took some pictures, spent a few minutes thinking about Graham, and began the descent back to my camp. Somehow I could see Graham's spirit residing on that mountain, looking over the place he had visited so many years ago as a young man. This was an impossible notion, perhaps, but comforting nonetheless to me at the time.

This mountain reminded me of another that I'd climbed alone a summer or two previously, in the beautiful Alps near Lech, Austria. On the summit of that unnamed peak, I'd dedicated the moment and the mountain to Graham as well. Then, a few years later, I climbed the "real" Graham Peak, a 12,500-foot mountain in the San Juan range in southwest Colorado. I'm not sure I'll ever stop climbing or dedicating mountains to my son's memory.

I descended Graham Mountain into the wooded valley below. It grew darker, both with the dusk and the tall trees. I lit a few small, dry twigs to begin my evening's fire. As the flames grew, the light, warmth, smell, and sounds transformed the damp forest into a cozy spot. This would be home for tonight, and a fine home it was.

I sat on the ground and cooked my dinner, a simple process of heating water on my tiny gas stove and then pouring the boiling water into a pouch of freeze-dried food. It was tasty and filling. After eating, I settled into my accustomed position, leaning back on a tree and getting as comfortable as possible on the hard, cold ground and the straight, rough tree. This was my easy chair, night after night. In it I would sit and ponder the fire and the things that I had experienced over those eighteen days in the wilderness.

I thought back to one of the first mornings of my trip. I had set out on a grass-and-wildflower-lined trail that led me out of a steep valley. The trail was very wet and muddy from a long rain the night before, which had confined me in my tent from before sunset to after sunrise. I had been happy to be back on the trail as the sun began to dry and warm my surroundings. Most of the time, I'd trudged with head bent so I could see the obstacles as they came toward me on the trail. Sweat had dripped into my green bandana. I thought about the trail, the push of my muscles, and the pull of the earth's gravity.

On that day I glanced up at the stark blue sky. Just above the western horizon hung a pale moon, barely visible in the bright morning sun. It reminded me immediately of seeing the moon in the same position in the morning sky just a day or two after Graham had died more than three years earlier. The sight of that moon gave me the same awful, empty, sad feeling. For the first time in a long time, perhaps a year or two, I wept. I simply stopped right there on the trail, dropped to one knee, bowed my head, and sobbed.

Eventually, the fire began to die out, and my thoughts shifted from my previous days on the trail to the cold. I had no more dead branches by my side, so I decided to get my aching body up and into my warm sleeping bag. I walked out into the dark forest to relieve myself before going to bed. As the fire died down to glowing embers, the absolute dark of the night became more real. The irregular glow of the Milky Way swept across the top of the sky from north to south in a subtle display of immensity.

I had spent considerable time thinking about what I did or failed to do to keep my son alive. This can be an endless and agonizing line of thought. There are many possibilities to consider, and consider them I did—at length. In the end, however, I had no real choice but to conclude I could never figure out what had happened to my son or why. Just as certain and real was the fact that I couldn't fix it. So I asked myself, why keep trying? What was the point in that? Who was that helping?

Now, for a moment, I felt at peace with the world and myself. Briefly I knew that some questions would never have answers; that the world was much too complex and mysterious and unknown. Briefly it was enough just to stand on the dark side of this planet as it spun through space and feel that I was alive. Briefly it was enough to just see the cycle of life and death unfold around me everywhere by day, to hear it at night. These natural cycles were exactly the same as my own, the cycle that would inevitably lay claim to my own body. I could see it all unfolding, slowly but surely, right before me.

In a world preoccupied with the supernatural, I found myself that night under the night sky, simply standing there in the natural world, accepting my fate.

"Beyond here lies nothing, nothing but the moon and the stars."
— Bob Dylan, *Beyond Here Lies Nothing*

Chapter 43:
ABOVE THE WILDERNESS

Later the same summer in which I had replicated Graham's Outward Bound trip, on a flight from San Francisco to Denver over the Rocky Mountains, I tried again to put it all together, to put an end to my mind's restlessness.

From my window seat I looked down upon the same mountains where I had taken my eighteen-day backpack trip. I studied them and tried to find the valleys and mountains I had hiked, and thought about what I might have experienced down there, some thirty-five-thousand feet below my perch in the sky. Now the mountains that had seemed so big to me, so arduous to climb with my heavy pack, looked like mere bumps on the planet.

What could be so wonderful about trudging over those bumps, I asked myself. How could that possibly change the way I thought, the way I felt about my life? In contrast, the airplane seemed like a far more majestic perch from which to ponder the nature of things, removed from the sweat, the rain, the sun on my head. Maybe in the clear sky I could better perceive the nature of my own life and death, the nature of everything else that surrounded me, all I'd seen and would never see. Then clouds appeared, sweeping in below the plane, obscuring the mountains as if to hide them from my sight and mind.

And with the clouds, my own thoughts slipped into disarray again, whatever lessons I'd learned on the trail gone. I reflected on the fact that I was trying to put it all into some kind of order that made sense, so I knew what had happened to me, what might happen to me, and why. Why did these things happen, and why did they happen to me in particular? There must be some kind of explanation.

And if there were no explanations, then how could I be sane? What was preventing me from slipping into insanity? It seems too easy to let my mind slide in that other direction, the direction of disorder and nonsense, of no reasons and no answers.

I realized that I could make things up, and that worked for a while, but at the end of the day it was still made up by me, of all people. It didn't satisfy all the questions knocking around in my head. I couldn't make these things up, because I didn't know the answers any more than the next guy—and he obviously didn't know any more than I did. It was pretty obvious—yes, obvious.

So why had I hiked the hell out of my body down there, I asked myself. I didn't know. It was all good adventure, perhaps, and maybe that was all that mattered. But I wasn't that happy on the trail; I was merely distracted from my pain. I could only be truly happy if there were some meaning in it all, I thought. If I could discover just one fact or understand one feeling— just one—I would be content. I was a rational man, after all, I thought. That was all I need, just to understand something.

But in all my walking around and sleeping out under the stars, I hadn't found that fact. Maybe it wasn't in the wilderness. Maybe I'd been silly and childish, I thought, to believe it was out there at all. As if I were a lifetime member of the Boy Scouts of America, for God's sake. Where was *something* that would give some purpose and direction to my life, some order to the universe that I could find useful? If only there were some way to see that life isn't really that fragile, that there is something underlying it all that could soothe my sense of personal fragility.

I guessed there was no point in looking for something that wasn't there. I might as well just relax, take it easy, and drink a beer, I thought. Enjoy nature, enjoy it even though I didn't know why. Just get in a car and drive real fast down a road and not think about anything but the speed and the feel of the wind on my left arm. What could it hurt? I was going to face some pretty bad shit during the rest of my life, and then one day I was going to walk into a doctor's office and he'd tell me I had prostate cancer and would be going to heaven in a couple of months. And I didn't even believe in heaven. So I might as well drive around—not hike around—while I could. What was the point of walking around down there trying to figure things out, really?

As these thoughts swirled around in my head on the airplane, I wrote in my journal,

You think that you're going to write about all this, and that will make it all magically clearer. All this will happen right as the words leave your mind, then your fingers, and pop up on your computer screen. But as clever as you make yourself sound at times, it still doesn't get the job done. There is still this very unfinished business of coming to conclusions that might be of some assistance in preventing the slide to insanity, that insanity that seems closer all the time.

The writing seems an awful lot like the walking. It feels good at the time and seems purposeful, but at the end of the page or the end of the hike there doesn't seem to be much of a change in the only thing that I can change in this world: myself. I'm still the dulled and desperate person I was at the top of the page or the beginning of the hike.

I suppose it all gives you some kind of hope, false though it may be. There

is that brief feeling that it is okay, and that it will be okay. And because it can't be any other way, that acceptance even feels hopeful. That's a pretty sorry definition of hope for you, but it is something greater and better-feeling than despair, or the insanity you seem to be fighting.

I looked out the window of the plane, and the clouds were now gone. Now, wasn't that a nice metaphor for my plane ride back home, I thought wryly. They had been lifted, Praise the Lord. All was clear, up here in the plane in the sky looking down on the trails winding through those mountains. I could see it all so clearly from my seat flying through the great expanse of nothingness. It was suddenly and seemingly irrevocably clear, as clear as anything on this planet.

"Above the planet on a wing and a prayer my grubby halo, a vapour trail in the empty air. Across the clouds I see my shadow fly out of the corner of my watering eye. A dream unthreatened by the morning light could blow this soul right through the roof of night."

– Pink Floyd, *Learning to Fly*

Chapter 44:

PURPLE MOUNTAIN

When Graham was just fourteen years old, he took a Colorado Outward Bound course in the Elk Mountains just west of Aspen. It began June 21, 1996, and ended 18 days later on July 8. He would spend three of those days camping by himself. The other fifteen days were spent either with adult leaders or with about eight other young men (boys really) his age. They tromped around the rugged mountains, sleeping out at night under tarps. They had no campfires or any of the other comforts that he had been used to when he camped with our family, like ample food, flashlights, and toilet paper.

As parents, we thought this experience would be good for Graham. He was struggling to find himself, and we thought there would be no better place than the mountains of Colorado. If there was one place that Graham seemed happy and healthy, it was in nature.

He agreed that the adventure sounded like something worth doing. He got into shape for it, and we all nervously prepared for the day he would leave. It was the first time he would be away from home for any significant amount of time, and his first summer camp of any kind (except for an annual basketball camp with his mother and brothers in Kansas).

The time came for Mary and me to drop him off at Denver International Airport (DIA), where he met a leader and his group. From there they drove a van some five hours west, up into the high continental-divide region of the Rockies.

More than ten years later, I discovered Graham's journal from this trip. Ironically, or maybe appropriately, I found it after I backpacked in the Elk Mountains. And though Graham's journal was spotty and sometimes disjointed, it contained invaluable snapshots into my son's mind.

His first entries:

June 21, Day One

One of the most emotional and thoughtful days of my life. Probably among the top three most nervous days. The trip from the airport to the camp near Crested Butte took about six hours. I was tired for part of the ride. I sat by myself and didn't talk to anybody. We got to camp and met our instructors and got equipment. We went to sleep under a tarp and it rained the rest of the night. Today was a VERY big day for me. BIG DAY.

Day Two

I thought a lot today and I'm still very homesick and scared.

Day Three

Today was another huge day. I'm getting to know some of the kids in my group better. We hiked a lot and I got tired. We stayed up. I'm doing good with my equipment, but my pack is huge. Very thoughtful and emotional day. I felt very sad and missed my family, pets, and home very much. Issued ice axes.

Day Four

Today was the first day of my tears, besides on the bus from DIA. I was very frustrated, because I couldn't seem to understand some knots that we were learning. I was behind most everybody. I worked so hard that my hands got so dry that they started bleeding. I really have had some bad thoughts, and I don't feel good about myself at all. On the upside, I am getting to know my fellow patrol members a lot better. I've worked up enough courage to actually chat with them a little bit. I am still establishing an image of myself for my instructors and fellow students to see me as. It's going pretty good. Still feeling bad and lonely and homesick but better.

Then, later in his trip, Graham laments about not keeping up with his journal:

I am very sorry and feel VERY bad that I have not wrote (or could it be "written?") for so long in my journal. I just haven't had a lot of time these past four or five days. I hate myself for this and have beat myself up so hard that I have cried. I am SO sorry and whenever I think about not writing in my journal for a while I get that bad feeling in my chest and I feel like hurting myself or crying. All I can say to sum this up in one line is: SOMETIMES I REALLY REALLY HATE MYSELF.

Later, in the middle of the trip, he writes of his experience with technical climbing, in which he needed help setting up the fixed line:

I can get basically perfect grades in school and understand some things that some high school students can't come close to understanding, yet I can't tie knots that stupid people can tie. I've thought the preceding thought a million times and kicked myself for the idea of it and what it states. I have cried thinking this thought, and for the rest of this course I will probably keep repeating this thought and continue to hate myself for it.

We weren't going to climb up rock; we were going to climb up VERY steep snow. I did this surprisingly very well (not to brag). I felt bad because everyone else had failed to recognize my well-doing. I still felt pretty good, though. After reaching the top we ate another non-filling, non-satisfying lunch and began our descent. Our descent was long and tough because we couldn't go just straight down. It was too steep. We walked down a ridge and gradually descended the rocky, slick, snowy mountain. We got back to camp and packed our bags. We then hiked about four miles in about four hours. This hike was solid, mainly because it was a road and it was all flat or downhill. We looked [at] the map a lot and finally found the almost perfect site for camp for that night. We had a fairly good dinner (beans and rice) and went to sleep. I was the leader the next day so I had to wake everyone at 5:00 a.m. It was tough but I did it, kind of. Today was a satisfying day. We all worked hard and got a lot done.

On July 3, he set out for a two-night solo away from his group, alone in the wilderness. He talks about setting up his camp with a single tarp:

While I was doing all this tarp stuff I had several brief crying episodes thinking about home and mainly because I hate myself so much for reasons I'd rather not write about. If I could I probably would've cried all night but I controlled myself. It was hard, but I controlled my feelings, kind of.

He went to bed and awoke on July 4:

Today is my full day of solo. It is a thoughtful day and a day without words but with many feelings. A day that when it becomes dark I will know that my family is doing one of my favorite family activities, without me. I will cry today. It is Independence Day, the Fourth of July, and I wish so much that I could see my family. One bad thing that I will keep realizing no matter what is that I miss them, my family, a lot more than they, my family, miss me. They have one person to miss. I have five people, two dogs, two ferrets, a cat, many friends, a great home, sports, food, and MUCH more. All they have to miss is ONE PERSON. What makes it worse is the date of today. July Fourth. A day for the three Fs, Family, Fireworks, and Fun. Family being the most important one. Oh, yes, now I remember there being four Fs. The last one being Food, which I could definitely use right now.

I'm writing this entry in the afternoon of July 4, while my family is probably getting ready to grill hot dogs and hamburgers and have a big, happy family dinner. While they may also be under a huge tent or tarp now, buying fireworks for tonight. Maybe even at a parade or doing something with friends. My brothers, laughing and playing together while my parents care for them so well. While I sit here crying, making my own shelter, hurting with wounds and bites, eating three meals consisting of half a handful of raisins and peanuts and a cracker. I have no shower, no bed, no kitchen, no television, no basketball, no FAMILY. I am crying and depressed. My heart and chest literally, physically ache because of my great emotional pain. I will probably NEVER forget this day.

Well, this morning I woke up fairly late, I don't know what time it is because solo rules prevented me from taking my watch with me. I woke up, thought for a little while, then got some water down by the stream. After that I ate my ration and then wrote in my journal. Sometimes I would just stop writing in my journal and think. After writing a huge amount about day thirteen and thinking about a whole ton of things for a long time, I got tired and took a nap for I don't know how long. I got up from my nap and thought some more about more things. I went to get more water. I then thought more, then ate a very small lunch, my ration. After that I started writing in my journal and have been doing that since now. For the rest of the day I have one more thing specifically planned. That is to write a letter to myself. Valeri, one of the group leaders, told us that we could write a letter to ourselves, addressed to ourselves, give it to Outward Bound, and they will send it in six months. I think this is a very good idea and I'm going to do that. I've thought about what I'm going to say and everything. I have plenty of time to do this also. Luckily, it hasn't rained today so far. So right now I'm going to write that letter to myself.

I just finished that letter to myself about two or three minutes ago. It ended up being ten pages long and I am proud of myself for doing such a useful thing. It took me at LEAST an hour and a half, probably more. I never stopped writing once except a few times to cry and another to get more water. So, basically, I've been writing and relaxing all day. By the way, that Gookinaid stuff ain't half bad. I plan to eat some dinner, maybe write some more, drink water, think, and then hit the hay early again.

Earlier in the excursion, on June 25, which was Will's birthday, he wrote:

Today I cried almost immediately after I first glanced at my watch, realizing it was Will's birthday. I wish I could be there [at home] today or at least tonight. I really, REALLY hope he has an especially good birthday to make up for me not being there. I'm going to get him an extra-special, extra-late present. I love him a lot more than he thinks and I care about him so much. He's my closest brother in age (even though he's not very close) and he's very special to me. I wish I could be home today and give him company SO much. I LOVE YOU, WILL.

Today was somewhat of a big day. We climbed a mountain called Purple Mountain or Mount Purple. Everybody thought it was a huge thing, even though the mountain wasn't even thirteen thousand feet. The beginning of me being real frustrated with our pace came today. Our whole group seems to move VERY slow and it seems that we are taking a break every three steps. There are two kids that we are constantly waiting up for. I had some tears today for a few reasons. Mainly, Will's birthday. I am REALLY bummed about that. Another is because I greatly miss being with my dad up in the mountains. I miss him being with me in the outdoors SO much. I cried because I missed home and my family and there was nobody to talk to or to comfort me. Today wasn't that big of an Outward Bound day. It was a big day because of Will's birthday, though. I can't stop thinking about that. So, today we climbed Purple Mountain and that's about it.

"When I am down, and oh my soul so weary...you raise me up, so I can stand on mountains."

– Josh Groban, *You Raise Me Up*

Chapter 45:

PURPLE MOUNTAIN REVISITED

Years later, Will wrote back on Graham's birthday. As Graham had missed Will on his birthday back when he was camping in the Elk Mountains in 1996, Will missed Graham on August 7, 2006, when Graham was no longer with us. I didn't know about the letter until I later found it stuffed in a box of the boys' things in our basement.

Standing alone in the quiet basement, I read the letter. I smiled to myself as I saw the opening line, "u coo," which in the cryptic language of the boys from their earlier years meant "you are cool." I stood there remembering how the boys would constantly amuse each other with silly shorthand. Often they would use hand signals as they talked, spelling out the U with their thumb and index finger and so on through entire words, giggling and carrying on, having the times of their lives in such a simple way.

So, the short letter from Will began in the same manner these brothers had greeted each other with for years:

u coo 8/7/06

Happy 25th, Brah!

This isn't the type of card I ever thought I would be giving you on your fuckin' twenty-fifth B-day, man. Twenty-five. I know our relationship would be much different. How I miss it, the opportunity, to have grown w/ you as a brother and friend. It pisses me off more than anything. The family is just not the same without you. Time (the Pink Floyd song) just came on my iPod, one of your favs, I think. It would be so much fun to talk music w/ you...you would probably make fun of most of it, but I would love it. There is a hole that will never be replaced, just as you will never be forgotten. I love you so much and miss you so much and feel so bad for you and me and our family. I think of you every day and love you so much and will forever. Love you, bro, happy B-day.

—Will

Brother Will would go on to suffer his own depression. When he was studying in Barcelona a couple years after Graham's death he had what I would call a breakdown and began seeing a doctor there who prescribed the common anti-depressant, Effexor. This drug seemed to work for Will and he gradually improved, although he had to continue taking rather high amounts of the drug to adequately stave off the demon depression. While it broke our hearts as parents to see another one of our sons suffering this disease, at least Will appeared to be more receptive to medications than his older brother had. Will leads a fairly happy and normal life, where his easy-going and easy-to-love personality can continue to shine on to his countless friends and admiring family.

In the summer of 2009, thirteen summers after Graham's experience in the Elk Mountains and the fifth summer since he left us, Will and I backpacked from Maroon Lake near Aspen up to Maroon Pass, to the southwest. There, at twelve thousand, five-hundred feet, we could stand and look west over the entire area where Graham spent those eighteen days as a very young man in 1996, and where I had spent eighteen days the previous summer.

And as we pulled on our jackets against the sharp wind that whistled over the pass, we scanned the horizon. We both knew what we were looking for.

"I think it's that one, Dad, over there," Will said to me, pointing west and a little south. "It's got to be."

There was silence as we both squinted into the western sun, searching the horizon.

"It's beautiful," I said.

We pulled out the map to confirm our hunch, positioning it with the compass to make sure. We matched the contours of the map with the high, broad sweep of the summit we saw with our own eyes. It was the mountain that seemed to reach the highest, rise the most gracefully to the sky. The setting sun gave a pale, ethereal yellow glow to the air that surrounded the mountain, a heavenly halo.

This was the Purple Mountain that Graham had climbed so successfully all those years ago, missing his family all the while.

Now his brother and his father stood before the sacred mountain like two emissaries sent by his family to bid him adieu. We were quiet and contemplative, thinking not so much about the mountain's extraordinary, brilliant beauty, but rather remembering our Graham, who was, for this father and brother, the truly extraordinary, brilliant, and beautiful one.

"When he shall die, we will take him and change him into little stars, and he will make the skies above so fine that all the world will be in love with night."
– Adapted from William Shakespeare for Graham's memorial service program

Chapter 46:

UNDER THE NIGHT SKY

On Thanksgiving 2010, our family gathered at our mountain vacation home in Breckenridge, Colorado, a house Graham never saw, because we didn't purchase it until November 2007. As with every holiday gathering of our family, the atmosphere was bittersweet. Of course it was wonderful to have our children with us. Our boys are everything for Mary and me, and we love nothing more than to share time with them.

The bitter part was assembling as a family since February 2005 without Graham. His absence has never become less noticeable or less painful. His spirit was in the room every time we got together, and this was particularly the case when we gathered for holidays.

What was different was the new life in our small family. Will's long-time girlfriend, Tara, was nearly eight months pregnant, and her midsection bulged beautifully with the presence of the baby boy growing inside her. Always lovely, Tara had become beautiful with a mission, the most important kind of mission I could imagine. She was going to have a baby, the first grandchild in our family. We didn't know it then, but his name would be Walden Graham.

As we stood around the numerous platters of Thanksgiving food, we formed a circle and held hands. In our family's tradition, we took turns saying out loud what we were thankful for. Everyone mentioned family and friends, but also said how much they missed Graham. Colin's eyes filled with tears as he talked about his brother.

When my turn came, I simply said I was most thankful for my family, all eight of us now. Of course, two of us could not be seen, one who provided the hope and promise of the future, the other the sadness and sense of loss.

It was more than five years since Graham had passed away. Life had continued and changed.

Will and Tara had purchased and moved into a downtown Denver loft with a view of the magnificent skyline. They started their careers and fully enjoyed the urban life at their doorstep. In the New Year, their lives would change dramatically with the birth of their new baby boy, and they were excited about that. Walden Graham Stingley would be born on January 2, 2011.

They each remembered Graham in their own ways. Will busied himself with such projects as a walk for depression awareness in Washington, D.C. He put his computer skills and extensive social network to good use, raising money for the walk and spreading the word about the scope and seriousness of this disease. Will talked of doing even more to help those suffering from depression, perhaps even as a counselor at the newly opened Depression Center at the University of Colorado Medical Center in Denver.

Tara has been a respectful, quiet bystander to the grief that struck our family and an unflagging emotional support for Will through this most difficult time. Like all of us, she has both regrets and beautiful memories. After reading a draft of my book, Tara wrote me a long e-mail:

Your family is part of who I am, and I have always regretted not knowing Graham on a deeper level...I often think of one day in particular. We were barbecuing at the Lodgepole house, and Will, Graham, and I were sitting out on the deck. It was late summer I think, sunny and just starting to cool off. Will went inside, so it was just me and Graham. We talked a little, but I wish I could go back and really talk about the things that mattered to him or just go back and be in that moment, just to sit. I feel so lucky to have known him even the little bit that I did. His brilliance radiated from him; I think it intimidated me because I knew he understood things in a way that I couldn't.

It was heartbreaking to glimpse his depression through your memories and his journal entries. But it also gives me a sense of peace to better understand who he was.

Seth had recently moved to Palmer Lake, Colorado, just eight miles from our home in Monument. His Victorian house was in an eclectic neighborhood up against the Front Range of the Colorado Rockies, just a short hike away from our favorite local mountain, Mount Herman. He enjoyed taking long walks in the evenings after work with Ralph, a calm and curly specimen of a dog that looked loyally up to Seth with his big, brown eyes.

I shared several night hikes with Seth, as he led me up the same mountain trails I had run a thousand times over the years. Now that winter had come, these hikes were under cold, black, starry skies.

This was a neighborhood Graham had known well. He'd been a pizza delivery boy here, then later spent a lot of time at a house "in the glen," where his band's drummer lived with his wife. After Graham died, they sent us pictures of their new baby daughter. They gave her the middle name of Winter, Mary's maiden name, to honor Graham.

Seth found it difficult to talk about his dead brother, but I could hear his pain through his words. "I love to hike at night," he told me recently. "It's so beautiful and quiet and peaceful out there at night, unlike any other time."

And during the days, Seth took his thoughtfulness and search for peace to the roads, cycling for hundreds of miles all over Colorado. At times, he entered races, some over high mountain passes, some on the roads along the Front Range, one a climb to the top of Mt. Evans, which stands over fourteen thousand feet above the Front Range. When he was competing in pro-like events and there was a space for the team name on the entry form, I noticed he wrote, "Team Graham Stingley."

Looking one day at several journals for an entry of mine, I instead stumbled upon one of Seth's journals. He wrote extensively about Graham's influence on his life, and his continued love and respect for his brother. In an entry dated September 15, 2009, Seth wrote:

"I am thankful for my oldest brother, Graham, for teaching me, in life and death, that there is beauty in life and not take that for granted."

Colin, our youngest, who was twenty-one on that Thanksgiving Day, was about to graduate from the University of Colorado–Boulder, just as his two older brothers had done. Like them, he didn't talk about Graham that much, because, I think, it was just too painful to do so. Six years younger than Graham, Colin had had a unique relationship with his oldest brother from the beginning, and that bond was getting stronger just before Graham passed away. I remember them hanging out together in our study, listening to Coldplay, talking about music.

Now Colin had his own way of expressing his love for his brother, writing the letter G on almost any available material. One morning, when I awoke in my hotel room in Denver, I opened the curtain and noticed a simple G written in a smudge on the window. Colin had been there the night before to take me to a Roger Waters concert at the Pepsi Center. Days later, I saw the same G written in the dirt on the back of Colin's black car, by the same finger. And when I skied down from our house to the Breckenridge ski area a half hour after our boys had gone skiing, there was a G written with a ski pole in the fresh snow on the side of the trail.

Skiing was one of the things all our boys enjoyed. They all started at an early age and became expert skiers and snowboarders. I still remember Graham leading the way when the boys were young, skiing through the trees ahead of his brothers, then shooting out onto the open run and speeding down the hill far ahead of me. I know his brothers remember those wonderful times with their oldest brother every day they spend on the mountain.

We all remember in our own ways. We all have our own thoughts—and feelings.

Mary, smiling amid the activity and love of our Thanksgiving family gathering, turned to me at one point in the evening and said, "Graham would have loved this." Her smile turned down, and a tear ran down her cheek.

As for me, I have written enough, and I want to go on and not think, but just feel. I want to remember and be happy that I was fortunate enough to have twenty-three years with my son Graham.

Toward the end of that Thanksgiving night, I stepped outside to clear my head. I walked up the driveway and into the dark street, the snow crunching under my boots. I stopped in the middle of the street and looked back at the house, where I could see our family milling about and chatting with each other in the candlelight. Then I looked up. On this moonless night, at ten thousand feet and with no city lights, the night sky was ablaze with a billion stars.

"Yes," I whispered to myself. "Graham would have loved this."

"Say you finally invented a new story of your life. It is not the story of your defeat or your impotence and powerlessness before the large forces of wind and accident. It is not the sad story of your son's death....it is a story...of prose and enduring love...you have been writing all your life...where you can rise from the bleak island of your old story and tread your way home."
Michael Blumenthal, *The New Story of Your Life*

EPILOGUE

From somewhere in the house—I can't tell where—come the muffled cries of a distraught mother. The sobs are familiar; I have heard them many times before, and I will hear them many times again. I follow the sobs upstairs, to where I think Mary has been getting dressed this early Monday morning. But as I walk up the stairs, calling her name, the sobs get quieter. I head downstairs, to the lower level of our three-story home, and the sobbing gets louder.

It is coming from behind the closed door of our workout room, where Mary spends almost every morning walking for an hour on the treadmill, watching TV. The TV is silent, but I hear Mary's quiet, awful sobs from behind the door. I call her name and she comes out, crying and red-eyed.

"I thought you were gone," she says, giving me the sinking feeling that if I hadn't been here, if I hadn't forgotten to check something on my computer, she would have been sobbing alone in this house.

She rushes to me and I to her. I hold her and she embraces me tightly. She sobs more deeply.

"Sometimes it is just unbearable," she says, very softly. "Sometimes I just don't know how to go on."

"I know," I reply. "I know."

We embrace silently there in the dark hallway outside the workout room for a few minutes. There is nothing else to say. There is nothing else that could be said. It is enough that we both can feel the same pain and hold each other through it.

"Did something in particular remind you?" I finally ask.

"Yes, it was the family picture in Will's room. It's covered up because he can't stand to look at it," she replies.

We both walk into Will's room, vacant now because he moved out just a couple days before. There, hanging above his dresser, is a triptych of pictures assembled by a friend who is a professional photographer. There was a picture of Will and me to one side, a picture of Will and his mother to the other side, and in the middle, covered by a subway map of Barcelona, the picture we can't see but know to be there: one of our entire family. The middle picture shows Mary, me, the three boys, and the two dogs. The whole family, that is, without Graham.

"See," Mary says, pointing to the picture. "He can't stand to look at all of us together without him."

Something similar had happened in Breckenridge. At our vacation home there I had hung a picture of the three boys taken after Graham's death.

Will had politely asked me if I would take the photograph down. We didn't discuss why. It is usually difficult for my sons and me to talk about these horrible feelings we have. Like the cobbler with the shoeless children, I can sit here at my desk and write about my grief, but it is next to impossible to talk about it with my sons. I don't know why, it just is.

EPILOGUE

I took the picture down and searched at home for a picture of all four boys, coming up with one taken when Graham was probably ten and Colin perhaps four. They are all dressed in their Sunday best and smiling happily for the photographer. I placed the photograph with its slightly scratched, black wooden frame upon the mantle in the living room, easy for everyone to see. It was as if I had put our family back together.

Graham looked particularly happy in the picture. He was dressed in a V-neck white sweater with a navy-blue stripe around the neck. Underneath, he wore a blue, button-down shirt. This photo captured a time when all the boys were young, innocent, and happy, before they encountered the complexities and difficulties of the world. It was a complete picture. A perfect picture: a picture with all four of my sons. This was a picture that anyone in our family could look at.

After I placed it on the mantle, Mary walked into the room. For what seemed like an eternity, she stared at the picture and then looked away, as if she were caught in another world. I continued to watch. Finally, she looked at me. There was really no emotion in her face, but a tear ran down her cheek.

"Oh, that picture," she said. "Oh, that picture is so beautiful."

Graham will never be photographed again. Not with a girlfriend, a dog, a baby, a wedding, a life. No more pictures of Graham.

We have boxes and boxes of photographs of him, his brothers, and his friends, from the 23 years of his growing up. Many of them show a very happy Graham enjoying his young life. Many of those photos are still trapped in the basement, but many we see now each day on our computer screens and our digital frames. And some pictures of Graham sit on his brothers' nightstands. Some even make it with us on our travels, pulled out of suitcases in faraway places and displayed in our hotel rooms.

Was it enough to have had Graham those twenty-three years, as some friends have urged us to believe? No, absolutely not. It will never be enough. But we can do nothing now about the fact that he is gone.

What we can do is be thankful that Graham lived at all and enriched our lives in countless ways. He showed us what it was like to be the firstborn son and oldest brother. And without intending to, he showed us how an innocent, intelligent and trusting young man searched for life's meaning, steadfastly optimistic that there were answers, even while bearing the burden of a debilitating depression.

He loved us and we loved him. So we go on with our lives the best we can, honoring his spirit and remembering his love, and continuing to love him for as long as we are alive.

And we make do with our memories, because that's our only choice, and our pictures that hold a precious fraction of the memories.

PHOTO GALLERY

*Photo courtesy of
d'Layne photography*

Starting top left and moving clockwise: A young Graham begins his lifelong love of music; Mary and the boys in Breckenridge; A toddler Graham with his best buddy, Willie; Mother and son.

Graham, right, with Will, learning to take care of brothers; Loving nature from the ground up; Fun with Pops and Will at Christmas; Before the big game.

Autumn in Lincoln; The arrival of Colin; Happy boy; Party time; Sunny days.

The whole family at Auntie's house; Feeding Seth; Father and son out for a hike; Going for a swim in the evening in Lake Michigan; The team; With Molly.

On the summit of a 14er; Cooking dinner; The gang at the water park; Backpacking with Pops; Backpacking with Scooter.

On the court as a sophomore; Relaxing in Jamaica; Learning guitar; Arriving at an alpine lake; Birthday morning on Cape Cod; High School Class of 2000; On the deck with Sally (Miss Masahi) and Scooter (Mr. Cooper).

The family at Fox Run Park; The boys; Happiness; For the 2000 yearbook; In Italy in 2004; On the Ligurian Sea 2004.

www.ingramcontent.com/pod-product-compliance
Lightning Source LLC
Chambersburg PA
CBHW022102090426
42743CB00008B/688